T O O
LATE

JYNEAN E. CHANDLER

Fulton Books, Inc.
Meadville, PA

Published by Fulton Books 2021

ISBN 978-1-63860-352-8 (paperback)
ISBN 978-1-63860-353-5 (digital)

Printed in the United States of America

CONTENTS

AN IMPORTANT WORD REGARDING THE RAPTURE

The next prophetic event that concerns the church and the true followers of Jesus Christ is known as the rapture. One day, soon, Jesus will appear in the clouds and call us up to be with him. He is currently preparing a place for us, and that place will soon be ready (John 14:2–3). Traditional pre-tribulation teaching is that this event is, and always has been, "imminent," in that it could happen at any time.

At the time of the rapture, believers who have died will have their bodies resurrected and, along with believers who are still living, will meet the Lord in the air. This will all occur in a moment in a twinkling of an eye.[1]

The rapture is described primarily in the books of the First Epistle to the Thessalonians 4:13–18 and the First Epistle to the Corinthians 15:50–54. God will resurrect all believers who have died, give them glorified bodies, and take them from the earth along with all living believers who will also be given glorified bodies at that time.

> For the Lord himself shall descend from heaven with a shout, with the voice of the arch-angel, and with the trump of God: and the dead in Christ shall rise first: Then we which are alive and remain shall be caught up together with them

---

[1] "What the Bible Really Says About the Rapture," Beliefnet, https://www.beliefnet.com/faiths/christianity/what-the-bible-really-says-about-the-rapture.

in the clouds, to meet the Lord in the air: and so shall we ever be with the Lord. (1 Thessalonians 4:16–17 KJV)

The doctrine of imminence, as it relates to Bible prophecy, teaches that nothing has to occur before the rapture of the church. Imminence means that Jesus could return at any moment, his return is impending, and it is ever near. The scripture teaches that we are to live in a state of constant readiness and expectation regarding the coming of the Lord. We are to watch. We are to be awake because the rapture could happen at any time. [2]

The rapture will involve an instantaneous transformation of our bodies to fit us for eternity. "We know that when he (Christ) appears, we shall be like him, for we shall see him as he is" (1 John 3:2). The rapture is to be distinguished from the second coming. At the rapture, the Lord comes "in the clouds" to meet us "in the air" (1 Thessalonians 4:17). At the second coming, the Lord descends all the way to the earth to stand on the Mount of Olives, resulting in a great earthquake followed by a defeat of God's enemies (Zechariah 14:3–4).

The doctrine of the rapture was not taught in the Old Testament, which is why Paul called it a "mystery" now revealed:

> Listen, I tell you a mystery: We will not all sleep, but we will all be changed—in a flash, in the twinkling of an eye, at the last trumpet. For the trumpet will sound, the dead will be raised imperishable, and we will be changed. (1 Corinthians 15:51–52)

The rapture of the church is a glorious event we should all be longing for. We will finally be free from sin. We will be in God's presence forever. There is far too much debate over the meaning

---

[2] "What the Bible Really Says About the Rapture," Beliefnet, https://www.beliefnet.com/faiths/christianity/what-the-bible-really-says-about-the-rapture.

and scope of the rapture. This is not God's intent. Rather, the rapture should be a comforting doctrine full of hope; God wants us to "encourage each other with these words" (1 Thessalonians 4:18).[3]

The doctrine of imminence, as it relates to Bible prophecy, teaches that nothing has to occur before the rapture of the church takes place. Imminence means that Jesus could return at any moment, *his* return is impending, and it is ever near. The scripture teaches that we are to live in a state of constant readiness and expectation regarding the coming of the Lord. Or will you be…left behind?

---

[3] "Are Our Rapture Bodies Real," Grace thru faith, published March 14, 2009, gracethrufaith.com/ask-a-bible-teacher/are-our-rapture-bodies-real.

ACKNOWLEDGMENTS

First of all, I give all the glory and honor to my God for giving me the unction to write this book. Even though it is a fictional novel, the theme and story line could happen to anyone. I targeted the teenage group because they think they have plenty of time to give their heart to the Lord or that they are invincible; however, I recommend all age groups to read this book.

There have been several family members and friends who have encouraged me in writing this novel. I would like to thank my dear husband, Pastor Jerome Chandler, for being my friend and "sounding board" regarding the story line and the themes of the chapters of this novel.

I want to thank my sweet mother, Louise Lockett, affectionately known as "Gammy." She used to always say that she was the "universal grandmother." She has gone on to be with the Lord, but she constantly encouraged me to pursue this endeavor. I shared the plot and the ending of the novel with her; she got so excited and told me she couldn't wait to read it. She would often say, "*Girl, hurry up and finish writing that book so I can read it. You know I will have it read in one day!*" Of course, she was right because whenever I bought a book from the bookstore, I always let her read it first, and sure enough, she would have it finished by the next morning. She was my inspiration, and I miss her so much.

I want to give a special thank you to my spiritual son, Michael Hastings, who really pushed me to complete this novel. He constantly called me on the phone asking when I was going to finish the novel because he was so anxious to read it as well. So, "Mike," I did it! I finally finished the novel!

I would like to dedicate this novel to my adult children: Evangelist Chantelle Hutchins of Charlotte, North Carolina; my son Pastor Jerome Christopher Chandler of Detroit, Michigan; daughter in love Angela Chandler, and my seven grandchildren Jerome Aslan, Jordan, Joshua, Grace, Derrick Zaccarion, and Rashidah.

INTRODUCTION

How did I, this fifteen-year-old girl, end up in this predica-ment? What could have possibly made me think I could escape such a tragic fate? I was one of those foolish people who thought they had enough time to give their hearts to the Lord. I have asked myself this question over and over again. Now, here I am (alone) without my mother who was in that group of Christians that were raptured. Why was I so foolish? Why didn't I make the choice to give my life to the Lord on that fateful night at our church's summer revival? My mom warned me that this day would happen, but I didn't want to hear it.

You see, several months ago, "the rapture of the church" from this earth to glory took place, and I have been left behind. Both the living believers and the dead in Christ were actually caught up to meet the Lord in the air, just like my mother constantly told me. And why didn't I listen to the visiting pastor, affectionately known as "Pastor Ray," who conducted that fateful revival at my church that forever changed my life.

I cannot believe that the rapture really took place, and I got left behind. The scriptures that Pastor Ray preached on that fateful night of the revival actually came to pass and (now) his words are a con-stant echo in my mind as I write in my journal. The scripture says:

> For this we say unto you by the word of the Lord, that we which are alive and remain unto the coming of the Lord shall not prevent them which are asleep. For the Lord himself shall descend from heaven with a shout, with the voice of the archangel, and with the trump of God: and the dead in Christ shall rise first: Then we

which are alive and remain shall be caught up
together with them in the clouds, to meet the
Lord in the air: and so shall we ever be with the
Lord. (1 Thessalonians 4:15–17)

However, I found out through Bible study that there will be
many people who come to Christ during the tribulation period.
Thank God, I have become one of those "tribulation Christians." I
read that there will be a countless number of people all over the world
that will get saved during this period (Revelation 7:14). The majority
of those of us who got saved during the tribulation period, however,
will die as martyrs. All of us will be the object of special persecution
by the leader of the one-world government, who is the Antichrist.
We know that we have refused to worship or receive the mark of the
beast based on Revelation 13:15. The result will be martyrdom. If we
meet this fate, the good thing is that we will be taken up to heaven
in the presence of the Lamb and God who will wipe away all tears
resulting from their suffering on earth (Revelation 7:14–17).

As I am sitting here writing in my journal, I have actually witnessed this event as well as see the rise of the Antichrist and his militia, just like Pastor Ray and my mother said. This man of perdition
started out speaking peace to the world when all seemed lost after
the rapture took place. He stepped in and miraculously brought
a false sense of hope to the world; however, I know who he really
is. Dr. Benetue Commeme is the Antichrist whom the Bible spoke
about. The world is in for a rude awakening. This man was elected
as our world leader and formed a one-world government who all of
the world leaders literally gave their allegiance, and they (readily)
accepted him as our new leader.

I cannot believe that world leaders willingly surrendered their
power to this man. He even sent out a decree all over the world that
all men and women are to wear his mark to show their allegiance to
him. I remember my mother telling me about the mark of the beast
"666," and I really didn't pay that much attention to what she was
trying to tell me. Now, it is so real; it's like I can hear her voice in my
ears telling me, *"Honey, please don't take that mark!"*

This man, Dr. Benetue Commeme, even went as far as confiscating all Bibles and have them burned and set up training, or should I say "deprograming" stations, for people who refused to take his *mark*. He set up an image of himself in the Universal Temple located in Jerusalem, requiring all people to pay homage daily to him as their new "savior." He (also) set up his headquarters right there where he daily broadcasts on the world social media giving what he calls "spiritual enlightenments for the day."

Because of the warning I received from my mother and the preaching of Pastor Ray, I realize that I am responsible for being in this predicament, and I decided to repent and give my heart to the Lord. Even though I have been left behind, I realize that I still have a chance. I must *refuse the mark of the beast* and *refuse to worship the Antichrist* or his image at any cost, according to Revelation 13:15–17. I also read in Revelation 14:11 that "*it is far better for me to suffer for a little while, now and soon be with Christ, than to escape suffering by yielding to the Antichrist and suffer the torments of hell, forever.*"

The Bible bears testimony that during this time, known as the "tribulation period," we can neither buy nor sell without the mark of the beast, which will bring great suffering and death to those who refuse the mark. *But he that receives the mark is eternally damned, and the wrath of the living God abides on him* (Revelation 13:15–17).

When the Antichrist introduced his mark, I am one of those believers who refused to take this mark no matter the circumstance, including threat of death. Revelation 14:9–11 says:

> A third angel followed them and said in a loud voice: "If anyone worships the beast and its image and receives its mark on their forehead or on their hand, they, too, will drink the wine of God's fury, which has been poured full strength into the cup of his wrath. They will be tormented with burning sulfur in the presence of the holy angels and of the Lamb. And the smoke of their torment will rise for ever and ever. There will be no rest day or night for those who worship the

beast and its image, or for anyone who receives
the mark of its name."

I read, from the notes my mother left me that once you take the
mark you are doomed eternally to death and the Lake of Fire.

I thank God that I am (now) with fellow believers who have
also refused to take the *mark of the beast*! We have been hiding out
in an obscure campsite because Christians are being rounded up and
given a choice of either taking this mark or be killed. There are many
of us here who have made this choice. We are all awaiting our fate,
which will inevitably be martyrdom. Any day, we are going to be
discovered and taken prisoner by these world leaders lynching men
and eventually be killed; however, we are ready to die for the cause
of Christ. I am no longer afraid. I know that I will soon see Jesus
face-to-face.

I am writing these words in my journal in case we have been
discovered. If I am martyred, I know I am going home to be with my
Savior. So if anyone finds this journal, and you have been left behind,
please know that you still have a chance. *Please read!*

CHAPTER 1

HOW IT ALL BEGAN
(BEFORE THE RAPTURE)

It all began that fateful morning (several months ago). I was lying in my bed, dreading even the thought of getting up to go to church. I could hear the birds chirping in the trees from my backyard and could feel a cool breeze blowing over my feet from the open window. I thought to myself, *Why are my feet so cold?* I soon realized that my feet had come out from under the covers. I quickly sat up in bed and reached down and pulled the covers back over my feet. I thought to myself, *Girl, you better get up before Mama comes in here singing that crazy song she made up—"Get up! Sleepyhead! Get up!"* I hated that song!

It was Sunday morning, and I had to get ready for church. This was a very special Sunday because it was the kickoff of our yearly "summer revival." However, instead of getting up, like my mind was telling me, my body was saying, *Stacie, roll over and go back to sleep.* I just had to get that last ounce of sleep, so I yielded to what my body was telling me to do. *Stay in bed!*

Suddenly, I heard the familiar sounds of footsteps coming up the stairs. It was my mom coming to wake me up for church. I swear, she always sounded like she was stomping on every step, which annoyed me to no end; and of course, she started singing that song I hated so much, "*Stacie, get up! Sleepyhead! Get up!*" She began to scold me, "You know it's Sunday! We got to get moving." I replied, "I know, Ma! I know! I'm getting up." (Of course, I was lying—because I didn't budge.)

Finally, I managed to get out of the bed and made my way to the shower. I turned on the shower faucet and just stood there underneath the water and let that warm water run down my face and body. It felt so good and soothing. I just wanted to stay in that shower for a while and not think about anything else. I always felt like the water washed away all of my cares. But, as reality sank in, I knew I had to hurry up so I wouldn't be the one who made us late for church.

For some reason, I had a feeling that this was going to be an unusual Sunday because we had a guest pastor coming to speak at our church. His name was Pastor Charles Ray. He was a very good speaker, and my pastor (Rev. Ronald Moore) always invited him to conduct our yearly summer revival.

We had an average-sized church (Mt. Calvary Christian Center) that seated about 250–300 people. Even though I hadn't yet given my heart to the Lord, I loved to hear my pastor preach. And I, especially, liked to hear Pastor Ray preach. He really held our attention, especially us young people. I even remembered most of the sermons that he preached at our church almost every year, and I had to admit that I couldn't wait to hear him this morning; that was something to say coming from a teenager (of course, I wouldn't admit it to my mom).

When I finally got dressed and came downstairs, my mother had a nice hot breakfast waiting for the two of us at the table. I could smell the aroma as I bounded down the stairs and walked into the kitchen. She had hot grits with melted butter and cheese bubbling in a pot on the stove, maple-coated bacon (which was her very own concoction, and it was so good), scrambled eggs, and homemade blueberry muffins. My mom was such a good cook. My friends would often say, "I sure wish our mom cooked like yours."

I plopped down in my seat at the kitchen table, and my mom said the grace. After what seemed to be a very long prayer, I dived into my plate with my fork in my hand as though I was famished. My mom rushed me to hurry up and eat so that we wouldn't be late for service, so I gulped down my food, thinking to myself, *I sure would like seconds. I ought to sneak a couple pieces of bacon in my coat pocket to eat in the car (which, of course, I did).* After we finished eating breakfast, we didn't have time to wash the dishes, so we scraped our plates, ran some water over them, and placed them in the sink.

As we hurried to the car, which was parked in the driveway, I wondered if my friends were going to be at church so we could have fun passing notes and laughing at the way some of the older church members would shout and praise the Lord. But deep down inside, I (also) wanted to hear what Pastor Ray had to say.

For some reason, I had a fear about this particular sermon because he said he was going to be talking about "the end-times!" He had a way of making me feel convicted, "hell scared," and excited all at the same time. I hoped that my friends would be there because they would be a good distraction for me, and Pastor Ray's words would not pierce me in the heart like they always did.

Our church was about an hour from our house. All the while Mom was driving, she was giving me warnings of how not to act up in church. She just went on and on about respecting the house of God. It annoyed me to no end!

When we (finally) pulled into the church parking lot, I sensed that it was going to be an exciting day because there were cars and buses everywhere! People from other churches in our small town along with those who came from the surrounding cities had heard that Pastor Ray was coming to our church for the summer revival, so they brought busloads of their members. Needless to say, the church parking lot was full, and people were still coming. The parking attendants had their job cut out for them because the cars were wrapped around the block waiting to get into the lot.

Pastor Ray even brought his congregation, Holy Trinity Christian Church. I saw their huge bus parked in the lot as well. I thought to myself, *They had the "best" choir in the world!* I knew they were going to rock the church when they sang. I loved to hear that choir sing because they would always sing the latest gospel songs.

They had a lot of young people in their choir, and they seemed so sincere and always had the whole congregation up on their feet, clapping their hands, singing along with them, and shouting down the aisles.

When we finally found a parking spot, my mother and I hurried and got out of the car and made our way into the sanctuary. The greeters were on their posts in the vestibule welcoming everyone as they came in. I had to admit, some of the greeters did a wonderful job of making everyone feel so welcome. They had such a warm and inviting smile on their faces, and I loved to get a hug from them as we entered the sanctuary because it felt so genuine.

My mother usually sat in the mother's board and missionaries' section of the church. As we walked in, she whispered to me, "You can sit over there with your friends (in the youth section), but don't let me see you cuttin' up today, do you hear me?" I replied, "Okay, Ma! I won't." I was so glad she let me sit with my friends because I had a feeling this was going to be an unusual service, and I planned on having a good time clowning with my friends.

As I looked around the sanctuary toward the youth section, I spotted my friends motioning for me to come and sit with them. I was so glad that they saved me a seat; however, I was on the lookout for this usher by the name of Sister Bessie Chambers who (I felt) was the meanest usher in the world. I knew if she saw me, she would make me go right back and sit with my mother so that I would stay out of trouble. I thought to myself, *She makes me sick! I can't stand that lady!*

While I was still in the lobby, I noticed that the Holy Trinity Gospel Choir was lining up to make their way down the middle aisle toward the choir stand. I hurried up and filed in right behind them as if I was part of their choir. When they started walking down the aisle singing, I walked right in with them singing, smiling, and waving at the congregation like I was part of the choir. It was too funny. People thought that I was part of the choir. When I got to the row where my friends were sitting, they spotted me and saw what I was doing. They were hysterical in laughter. I quickly ducked in the row where they were sitting, cracking up laughing because I pulled off that stunt, and Sister Chambers (the usher from hell) didn't even see me.

Whew! (I thought to myself, *I made it! Girl, you are a genius!*) As I scooted down the row to the seat my friends had saved for me, they were laughing and sliding down in their seats. They couldn't believe I had the nerve to march in with the choir, waving and singing with them. We all got a good laugh out of that stunt. My friend Paul said, "Girl, you are stupid! I never would have thought to do that!"

As the service began, the Holy Trinity Gospel Choir finished making their way to the choir stand and sat down until it was their time to sing. The praise team from our church was first on the program after the opening prayer and scripture reading. They came from behind the platform and ran toward the pulpit area in high energy, clapping and singing with their microphones in their hands. It reminded me of a rock concert. Our praise team director, Brother Gary Redmond, was very gifted in staging and props. He had platform lighting complete with floodlighting on the stage and colored lights overhead. In the background, there was a multicolored screen with a cross and a Bible.

The congregation went wild and began to stand up all over the sanctuary as the musicians began to play. The praise team began to clap their hands and sing, inviting the congregation to join in. I had to admit, it was awesome, and I stood up and joined in as they sang some of my favorite songs.

After they led the church into a really great worship service, I had to remind myself, *Girl, you better sit down before you get too caught up in the worship atmosphere and embarrass yourself in front of your friends.* So I sat down and pretended that I was not enjoying the music.

As much as I tried to act like I was bored, the service was really on fire, and the Holy Trinity Gospel Choir didn't let me down either. They sang so well that all of my friends and I stood back up and joined in, clapping our hands and singing with them. Their choir director was "bad"; he gave me goose bumps. He directed that choir like it was his last time. I thought to myself, *I wish I could direct a choir like that one day.*

All of a sudden, I saw old mother Shaw running down the aisle. When she got to the front of the church, she began to dance and prance in the spirit. She reminded me of a horse prancing back and forth. I tapped my friend Rayna, and she squeezed my hand as we began to laugh and snicker under our breath. Then, Deacon Harris broke out in a dance and started shuffling down the aisle (sideways) from side to side like a penguin. It was hilarious! My friends and I were sick with laughter. I had tears coming down my cheeks. I knew I shouldn't have been laughing, but it was too entertaining.

People began to break out in an ecstatic holy dance shouting, "Hallelujah," and, "thank you, Jesus," all over the sanctuary as the guest choir sang. I thought to myself, *Let the show begin!* People broke out with tambourines, and the drummer played those drums totally lost in worship. I had to admit that I loved a lively church service. I hate visiting churches that are boring because they put me to sleep.

If my mother knew how much I was cutting up in church, I would have gotten popped or pinched. I kept looking around to make sure she wasn't watching me or if that "usher from hell" Sister Chambers had spotted our shenanigans. However, they were both so caught up in the atmosphere of worship that they didn't notice me or my friends acting up.

After the Holy Trinity Gospel Choir finished singing, our pastor, Reverend Moore, got up and gave a good introduction to our guest revivalist. Pastor Ray then got up from his chair (in the pulpit) and walked to the podium to deliver his "revival" message. I began to get nervous, and I could feel my heart pounding like it was going to jump out of my chest. The palms of my hands felt cold and sweaty. I knew he was going to preach one of those messages that made the church search their heart. I could see it on his face, and he had that eerie look in his eyes. He had such tenderness and concern for people, and it showed on his countenance. I was scared!

Pastor Ray began to say, "I bring holy greetings to everyone here this morning from Holy Trinity Christian Church! I am so glad to see all of you who have come from near and far to hear this little ole preacher give you a message from the Lord. We are going to be looking at some scriptures this morning that deal with a familiar subject, 'the rapture of the church' or 'are you ready?'"

I thought to myself, *Oh no, we are in trouble now. This is the scariest subject I have ever heard and read about.*

I may not have known everything there is to know about the Bible, but I did know that the preaching of the "rapture" always made me scared.

Pastor Ray polled the audience by asking a question: *How many of you know we are living in the last days?* (The majority of the congregation raised their hands.) I looked down the pew at my friend Jasmine. She had her hand up too. I leaned over and teased her for raising her hand in agreement with Pastor Ray. She defended herself by saying, "I might not be saved, but I do know these are the last days." She had a serious tone to her voice that made me realize we weren't going to have any more fun laughing at people, texting, passing notes, or anything like that with her. I leaned back in my chair and said to myself, *This is going to be a long morning.* I looked down the opposite direction at my other friends, and they gave me the "okay" sign indicating that we were on the same page, so I relaxed knowing that they weren't as serious as Jasmine, and we could still have some fun.

Pastor Ray began to speak with fire and excitement in his voice. He gave us his testimony of how, before he gave his heart to the Lord, he had sunk so low in sin. He had become a drug dealer and an addict. I was so shocked! *Not Pastor Ray! Wow!* He seemed to be the sweetest and most humble man I had ever met.

He shared how he sold drugs on the streets of Harlem, New York, and how he and his friends had a well-organized gang called the "Unifiers Fist." He explained how he was in his element as a dealer until he began using some of his own products and ended up addicted to heroin. He said that he began stealing and robbing from stores and breaking into elderly people's houses for money until he got caught and ended up in juvenile detention.

He went on to tell how that didn't stop him from getting into trouble again. As soon as he got out of juvenile detention, he just picked up where he left off selling drugs again until he ended up in federal prison at the age of twenty-one. He faced a mandatory sentence of five years for robbery because he was armed with a deadly weapon and possession of drugs.[4]

I kept saying to myself, *Not you, Pastor Ray! Not you!* He had me and my friend's total attention. It seemed everyone was glued to every word he was saying. He continued on to his testimony:

"While I was incarcerated, it was really hard. I would hear grown men crying in the middle of the night, and I was so scared because I knew they were being raped or beat up. When I was out there on those streets of New York, I tried to act like I was tough, thinking I was 'the man.' But, in prison, it was totally different. I got beat down just about every day by some of the gang members. They would walk up to you and demand all of your food and sometimes your shoes. I learned very quickly that you better not refuse.

"One time, I even got stabbed in my arm and chest for looking at this elderly man in the eye. He was one of the leaders in my cellblock, and he ruled it with an iron fist. No one was supposed to look him directly in the face because he felt like you disrespected his authority. I learned to be tough and formed my own gang, but deep down inside, I was a scared little boy. I often wondered, *How in the world did I let myself get into this situation?* All of the dreams and aspirations I had for myself disappeared when I began hanging around the wrong crowd. I let my grandmother down, and most of all, I let God down.

"One particular night, while I was in my jail cell, my roommate was reading the Bible. I often noticed that he kept to himself, and the inmates in our block had a deep respect for him. I asked him what he was reading, and he began to share the Word of God with me. I was so fascinated by the words that were coming out of his mouth. These were the same words that my grandmother used to say and read to me when I was a young boy. It brought back fond memories of my childhood. How I loved to go to church with my grandmother. I felt safe, and I felt the love of God surrounding me when I was with her.

"My own mother and father were not saved, and they lived a sinful lifestyle in front of me and my younger sister. All I saw them doing was drinking, snorting cocaine, and partying all night long

---

[4] Benjamin H. Hardy, Research Analyst, "OLR Research Report"

with their friends. These were the sad memories I had of them. Thank God I had a godly grandmother who would come and get me and my sister every weekend. I always felt like she rescued us from the pit of hell.

"Each night, my cellmate would share more and more about the love of Jesus, and I ended up surrendering my life to the Lord right there in my cell. He led me through the sinner's prayer, and I fell to my knees, sobbing like a baby, and surrendered my life to the Lord.

"When my five-year sentence was up, I felt like I walked away from bondage (literally and spiritually) into a brand-new life."

Pastor Ray had me and my friends on the edge of our seats as he continued:

"I began to serve the Lord by going back to those same streets in Harlem, New York, preaching the Gospel to all who would listen. Many souls got saved, and eventually, I was called to pastor and started Holy Trinity Community Church. I have seen people under the bondage of sin being transformed into the image of Christ. I have seen gangs bring their guns and drugs to the altar and exchange them for a Bible.

"Listen, people! God is sending out the 'clarion call.' People, please hear me! Jesus is about to crack the sky and come back to get his 'bride,' which is the church. The call has gone out for you to surrender your life to him. Will you be ready, or will you be left behind? Signs of the time are everywhere, and you must pay attention to what God is trying to say to you. He is saying, 'Get ready because I am coming soon.' The rapture of the church is imminent. Will you please listen to what I am saying?"

Pastor Ray began to teach on the subject of the rapture. He said:

"The English word *rapture* comes from the Latin word *rapio*, which means to seize or snatch in relation to an ecstasy of spirit or the actual removal from one place to another. In other words, it means to be carried away in spirit or in body. So the rapture of the church means the carrying away of the church from earth to heaven. [5]

---

[5] Rapture Ready, https://www.raptureready.com.

"Thus, there can be no doubt that the word is used in 1 Thessalonians 4:17 to indicate the actual removal of people from earth to heaven. The word *rapture* can also mean 'rescued before the tribulation.' The rapture miracle is going to happen, and it will catch a great multitude by surprise. Many of this world today find it hard to comprehend the rapture, and some mock or laugh at the idea of the rapture taking place. King Jesus Christ is coming, and we who are sealed and born-again (*new creatures*) Christians will be raptured from the face of the Earth before the Tribulation.[6]

"Plus, based on 2 Thessalonians 2:5–13, it clearly states that after the rapture of the church, Satan will unleash his deception or 'lie' on a worldwide scale to the point that he will explain away the rapture—in part by way of an 'alien' disclosure and direct contact.[7]"

He went on to say:

"I want you to know, brothers and sisters, that after the rapture has taken place, there will be many false stories and speculations about what happened to the raptured Christians. The things that I am about to share with you are real and will soon be a fact in your reality. Some people will have a tendency to just brush it off and say, 'That's crazy!' However, those who are left behind will remember what people like me warned them about.

"If you're too busy partying to even take heed to this warning, please keep a few copies of the Holy Bible in a safe place because they are going to be worth more than all the gold in the world. You better make sure you hold on to this message, take notes, and store it in your memory. Every second, the rapture of the church is getting closer. You will see more and future events pointing to this event. Nobody in their right mind would want to be anywhere on planet earth after the rapture because they are going to have to go through the terrible tribulation period.

"Hopefully, many of you will take heed today and believe and seek God. If you have any doubt that you're a Christian or you are in

---

[6] "Where did the term 'rapture' come from," Bible.org, last published January 1, 2001, https://bible.org/question/where-did-term-8216rapture%E2%80%99-come.

[7] 2 Thess. 2:5–15 (KJV)

a backslidden condition, it's time to get it right! Now is the time to repent and build a personal relationship with Jesus Christ! Don't let it be said, 'Too late!' Revelation 3:3 says, 'Remember therefore how thou hast received and heard, and hold fast, and repent. If therefore thou shalt not watch, I will come on thee as a thief, and thou shalt not know what hour I will come upon thee.[8]'"

After Pastor Ray preached his message, there was stillness all over the sanctuary. I could hear people sobbing and others with their hands lifted up toward the ceiling crying out to God. I felt numb and weepy, and for some reason, I couldn't keep my eyes off of him. My eyes filled with tears, and I felt as though he was speaking directly to me. I just sat there staring at Pastor Ray as he made the altar call. I felt like I was frozen! It felt like I could hardly breathe.

It looked as if hundreds of people got up out of their seats and made their way down the aisles to the altar. All of a sudden, I saw, out of the corner of my right eye, two of my friends, Paul and Jasmine, standing up (crying) and making their way to the middle aisle, and they began walking toward the altar. I could not believe my eyes! I felt betrayed and scared all at the same time. I thought to myself, *What just happened? They broke their promise that we were not going to be talked into getting saved today! I was glad for them but mad at them all at the same time.* There was a sick feeling in the pit of my stomach. I wanted to join them so badly, but something was holding me back. *I don't want to get saved yet!* I thought to myself. *I am only fifteen, and I have plenty of time to give my heart to the Lord. Besides, I haven't even had time to enjoy life and have fun, start dating, or even get married yet!"*

That thought process gave me a sense of relief, and I felt somewhat justified. But deep down inside, I knew I needed to be right up there at the altar with Paul and Jasmine. I didn't know what was hindering me. My legs felt like heavyweights, and I couldn't move, and my heart was racing. I watched as my friends fell on their knees, sobbing with their hands upraised toward heaven, and enthroned in worship. I whispered a little prayer under my breath, *God, I am not ready yet! I'm just not ready!*

---

[8]   Rev. 3:3 (KJV)

CHAPTER 2

SILENCE IS NOT ALWAYS GOLDEN

The ride home in the car was so quiet that you could probably hear a pin drop. I really believed that my mother was a little disappointed and annoyed with me because some of my friends got saved, and I didn't. She never looked at me while she was driving but stared out the front window as she clutched the steering wheel very tightly. I could see tears running down her cheeks, and I began to fidget with the button on my blouse and the frill on my sleeve because her quietness made me nervous. I felt so convicted and angry all at the same time.

After what seemed to be forever riding in the car, my mother broke the silence and finally spoke, "Stacie, honey, why didn't you want to get saved? I noticed some of your friends were touched by Pastor Ray's sermon and made the right choice to give their hearts to the Lord. What happened to you, honey?"

I felt very uncomfortable and angry because I knew she was right. I just didn't want to let her know what I was really feeling. I could have kicked myself for not making this important decision regarding where I was going to spend eternity. I replied (noticeably irritated), "Ma, I want to make up my own mind and not follow the crowd."

She replied, "But, Stacie, don't you know that the rapture can happen any day and if you are not ready, you will be left behind to face the terrible 'tribulation period'? Your friends made the choice to not be lost. I really wanted that for you as well, honey."

I just sat there with tears rolling down my face. I could taste the saltiness of my tears running in my mouth, but I didn't want to wipe them because my mom would have realized that I was crying. I made sure I had my head turned toward my window to hide my tears. I replied, "Ma, I know, I know! I am going to get saved soon. I'm just not ready right now! I know all about the rapture and the tribulation. We hear about it just about every other Sunday from Reverend Moore and tonight from Pastor Ray. Plus, you preach about it to me at home."

"Stacie, I love you, and I don't want you to miss the rapture. Honey, it is going to be awful! You will not be able to stand it!"

I replied, "Okay, Ma! I hear you! I hear you! I'm sorry I disappointed you!"

My mom replied, "You didn't disappoint me as much as you hurt yourself. Christ died that you might have life and to rescue you from the wrath to come."

Thankfully, we finally pulled into the driveway and into the garage. I was so glad to get home and go up to my room to try to get my mind off of the whole experience. I figured that I would watch a little TV and check my cell phone messages from my friends. Even though I enjoyed the choir and Pastor Ray's sermon, I just couldn't bring myself to get saved. I thought to myself, *What is wrong with me? Why didn't I just get up and go down that aisle to the altar? How could I have been so stupid?*

As I got out of the car and started walking toward the back door of our house, my cell phone rang. When I checked to see who was calling, it was my friend Jasmine. She Facetimed me so her face could appear on my phone. I didn't want to talk to her because I didn't want her to try to preach to me or make me feel ashamed that I didn't get saved, so I ignored the call and hurried up and pressed *end* so that the call would hang up.

As soon as my mother opened the back door that was connected to the garage, I hurried up and rushed past her and bounded up the stairs to my room. She yelled up the steps to me, "Stacie, come back down here a minute! I want to say one more thing to you." I turned around and went back downstairs to hear what my mother had to say, stomping down every step. She said, "Stacie, I just want you to know that I love you and that I don't mean to be 'preachy.' I just want you to go to heaven with me."

I replied, "I love you too, Mama. I promise you I will get saved soon."

As I ran up the steps to my bedroom, it felt like my "haven of rest." I was so emotionally drained that I just plopped down on my bed and pulled the covers over my head as if I were hiding from God. I didn't even bother to get out of my church clothes; I just kicked off my shoes. I cried and cried until I couldn't cry anymore. My mind kept racing and remembering the whole scene of Pastor Ray preaching and pleading for us to come to the altar. I couldn't get it out of my mind that my friends, my buddies, broke the oath we made to each other not to give in and get saved.

I tossed and turned practically the rest of the afternoon until I fell asleep. I didn't even wake up to eat dinner. I kept having nightmares about the whole church service and how I refused to get saved. Part of the time, I would wake up and sit on the side of the bed crying and would try to watch something on the television in my room to get my mind off of Pastor Ray's message, and then I would lie down again and attempt to get some sleep.

I don't know when I finally fell into a deep sleep or even how long I had been asleep. I just remember being awakened by the usual sound of birds chirping outside my window. I realized that it was Monday morning, and I still had my Sunday dress on complete with undergarments and stockings.

I also noticed that it smelled like something was burning on the stove. I thought to myself, *Now that is very unusual for my mother to burn food because she is such a good cook.* I jumped up and bolted down the stairs (taking two steps at a time) and called out to my mother, "Ma! Ma! Something's burning?" But there was no answer. There was chicken in the skillet burning on the stove and a pot of cabbage with potatoes that had burned to a crisp. Then I saw the most unusual thing: My mother's robe and underclothes were lying in the middle of the kitchen floor with her slippers underneath. She usually got out of her church clothes and would put on her robe and slippers while she cooked Sunday dinner. I thought to myself, *What in the world is this?*

I ran through the whole house looking for her calling her name. I thought to myself, *Where could she be? I hope she is not playing some dumb trick on me because this wasn't funny.* She was nowhere to be found. A fear came over me that was indescribable. I began to think in my mind, *Could she have been taken up in the rapture?*

I began to scream, *Oh no! No! No! Ma! Ma! Where are you! This is not funny!* I remembered how, sometimes, she would play little jokes on me and would hide and then jump out at me. I was hoping this was one of those practical jokes of hers. I ran to the closet by the front door and snatched it open (quickly), but she wasn't in there. I checked the bathrooms, and I even ran back upstairs to look in her bedroom and bathroom, but she was nowhere to be found.

I began to talk out loud, *I can't believe what I am seeing! Is this for real, or am I dreaming?* A fear came over me, and I felt as if I was going to have a heart attack. I thought to myself, *What am I supposed to do now without my mother to take care of me.* I dropped to the floor on my knees and began to cry bitterly. I screamed out loud, "*God, please don't let this be the rapture! Please! Please!*" I felt as though I couldn't breathe. I thought to myself, *I just can't believe this is really happening. This can't be true! Maybe my mother went to the store in a hurry and forgot to turn off the stove.*

Then, I had an idea, *If her car is gone, then she probably went to the store.* I ran to the back door that led to our garage and opened it, looking for my mom's car. *It was still there!* I slammed the back door so hard that the glass window shattered and large pieces of glass fell to the floor. One of the pieces of glass landed right on the top of my foot and cut a large gash in it. The thought came to me, *Just end it all and slit your wrist.* However, I couldn't bring myself to do it. Instead, I turned off the stove where the chicken and cabbage were burning and the coffee that was still brewing. I turned on the water faucet and grabbed a piece of paper towel, wet it, and wiped off the blood from the top of my foot. I held it on the cut until the bleeding stopped.

The house seemed so empty. I began to wander aimlessly throughout the house going from room to room still looking for my mother and hoping (somehow) it was all a dream and that I would suddenly wake up. I thought to myself, *Maybe if I turn on the news and there are no reports of people missing, I would be all right.* I walked over to the television and reluctantly turned it on.

As soon as the picture came to focus, there were words flashing on the screen: *breaking news.* A newscaster appeared, sitting at his desk with a look of bewilderment on his face. At the bottom of the screen was a continuous message playing as he was talking. The continuous message kept saying, "We interrupt this program for a special report, it seems that thousands of people have just vanished from the face of the earth!"

The newscaster began to say something that changed the course of events in history as I knew it!

"Ladies and gentlemen, there have been numerous reports coming in this morning that thousands of people have just vanished in thin air. We don't know what has happened, but our phones are lighting up as I speak, and people are panicking all over the United States. Wait! Wait! We are now getting new reports that this event has not just happened in our country but all over the world. It is total chaos!"

He then showed footage of people out in the streets looting, screaming, and crying, and cars piled up from numerous accidents as sirens and fire trucks were blazing down the streets of every major city and all over the world. It was pure madness.

The newscaster continued: "There have been reports of airplanes crashing to the ground because the pilots have vanished. Oh no! I just received another report that all of the babies in every nursery, hospital, and home around the world have vanished! What is going on, folks? I-I just don't know what to say! Our phones are ringing off the hooks, and we can't keep up with the calls. Is this what the Christians call 'the rapture of the church'? Have we been 'left behind'? Is it too late? Is this what the Christians have been warning us about? Stay tuned for further details."

As I sat on my living room sofa, I picked up one of the pillows and buried my head in it and began to cry in despair. I felt such a dread to even live. All of the memories of the Sunday school lessons and the sermons my pastor, Reverend Moore, taught and preached; thoughts of my mother warning me to get saved; and especially that fateful Sunday morning revival with Pastor Ray's sermon—all of these thoughts began to flow in my mind again. I missed the opportunity to give my life to the Lord because of my pride. How could I have been so *stupid*?

I began to feel hunger pains in the pit of my stomach, so I went to the kitchen and grabbed a slice of wheat bread to eat to keep up my strength. I reached in the skillet and fished out the chicken that had been burning on the stove earlier. It was burnt and full of grease, so I took a piece of paper towel and patted it down to get some of the grease off it and wrapped it between the slice of bread and ate it out of desperation.

All of a sudden, I began to feel light-headed, and the kitchen began to spin around. Later on, I realized that I must have fainted because I woke up lying on my back on the kitchen floor. I must have been on the floor for a couple of hours because it was well past 2:00 p.m. I sat up looking around trying to get my bearings. I thought to myself, *Was I dreaming, or is this real?"*

As I got up from the floor and got my bearings, I realized that I was not dreaming and that I was really on my own. The rapture really did occur, and I was "left behind." I thought to myself, *What am I going to do? How can I take care of myself on my own? I am only fifteen years old. I need my mother! Oh my god! Oh my god, this is for real!"*

I began to pace up and down throughout the house. I felt helpless and hopeless. I didn't know what to do, where to go, and who to even call. The sermon that Pastor Ray preached on that fateful Sunday morning kept coming to my mind. And I began to think about all of the times my mother would ask me questions about when I was going to give my heart to the Lord and how angry I used to get with her. Now, I wish she was here so that I could gladly say, "Yes, today I will."

CHAPTER 3

REALITY KICKED IN

The news was still on, and a female newscaster joined in. She began speaking about all the many disappearances of people and the utter chaos going on all over the world. They introduced a guest clergy who was being interviewed, and he was literally weeping on the TV screen. He began to explain that what people were saying was true and that the rapture did take place. I thought to myself, *Well, if the rapture took place, why are you still here?"* He was so passionate and contrite about what he was saying. He said, "My name is Pastor Goodman, and I want to speak to those of you whose loved ones have disappeared and are devastated."

He continued on to say, "I want you to listen to me carefully! An event called, 'the rapture of the church' has taken place, and we are left here to face one of the most terrible times ever experienced by mankind. I am a preacher. I have been pastoring my church for over forty years. I started out right with God. However, I got caught up with the megachurch culture. I began lusting after money, and I was full of self-righteousness. God kept sending me warnings, but I wouldn't listen. That is why God didn't take me. I am devastated, and I can only hope that I still have a chance to get it right." He was sobbing as the news commentator tried to console him, looking bewildered herself.

I got up from the sofa and walked to my front door. I needed some fresh air, so I walked out on the porch. As I stood there, I saw my neighbor, Mr. Anthony Lewis, sitting on his porch with his head in his hands looking as though he was distraught. Before I knew it, I walked down the steps toward his house, even though my legs felt like rubber bands.

As I made my way over to his house, I stopped in front of his steps and asked him if he was all right. He looked up at me and replied, "My wife and son just disappeared right before my eyes yesterday! They just vanished! I can't believe what happened! She and I got into an argument. She wanted me to go to church with her yesterday, and I refused. She started talking about that rapture stuff again. I was still angry at her, and so I threw a can of beer that I was drinking right in her face. All of a sudden, *poof*, she was gone! She vanished! She was holding our son, and he vanished too! Their clothes just fell to the floor, and they were gone! Is this what she constantly told me about 'the rapture'?"

He let out the most ear-piercing yell I had ever heard in my life. Then, all of a sudden, he stood up, jumped off the porch, and just took off running down the street like a madman. It scared me so bad that I turned around and ran back to my house as fast as I could. I just sat there on my own porch (heart pounding) wondering, *What will I do now? Who is going to take care of me? What is going to happen next? I can't live by myself! I am still a child. I need my mama! I need my mama!*

I remembered how Pastor Ray talked about what would happen after the rapture to those who got left behind and would have to face the wrath of the Antichrist and take the mark of the beast if they wanted to survive. *Is this really what I am about to face?* I thought to myself, *When will the Antichrist reveal himself to those of us who are left behind!* I ran back into the house and ran up the stairs to my bedroom, got in my bed, and pulled the covers over my head in terror.

I just lay there with the lights off, looking up at the insides of my covers for what seemed to be hours just thinking to myself, *God, what am I supposed to do now?* I wanted to kill myself, but I was afraid. I remembered how my mother used to warn me that it was not the answer and that if I did kill myself, I would end up in hell. So I turned over and drifted off to sleep.

When I woke up, I looked around in a daze, not knowing what time of day it was or where I was. When I realized I was in my bedroom and it was in the evening, I slowly got out of bed and walked over to my window to look at the night sky and the stars. It was funny how everything looked normal in the sky, and aside from police sirens and fire trucks racing down the street, everything seemed normal. I thought to myself, *Girl, you have been dreaming, and it's all a big nightmare.* I felt a sense of relief, but nervousness still lingered in my head, and my legs were still shaking from the scare I had earlier. I couldn't tell if I was dreaming or if it was real. I got back in my bed, afraid to face the fact that it might still be a reality.

The next morning, I woke up to the usual sound of birds chirping in the backyard tree. The sun was shining (as usual). We were on summer break from school, which meant I didn't have to get up early and get ready for school (thank God). Hoping I had been dreaming, I decided to take a shower and then go tell my mother what a horrible dream I had. I also knew I had to be prepared to hear her lecture me on the importance of getting saved before it was too late.

I got in the shower and let the warm water run down my face and my entire body as usual. It felt so good and therapeutic. I just stood there under the shower faucet and let the water rinse away the entire built-up trauma I was feeling. Yet, when I looked down at my hands, they were trembling, and I saw the big gash on my foot from the broken glass the day before. Reality slowly began to sink in that I had been "left behind," but I tried to ignore it.

I finally decided to get out of the shower and get dressed. I wanted to smell the aroma of breakfast cooking in the kitchen and feel my mother's loving arms wrapped around me, reassuring me everything would be all right.

After I got dressed, I had an eerie feeling in the pit of my stomach because I didn't hear my mother stirring around in the house. Usually, I would hear her singing while she cooked breakfast or at least hear the gospel radio station playing and her singing along with the music; however, there was dead silence in the house, and I couldn't smell anything cooking on the stove.

I bounded down the stairs looking for my mother (being in total denial). To my dismay, I didn't hear a sound. No food cooking on the stove, and the chill hit me in the pit of my stomach that my worst fears were reality. *I was not dreaming!* I began to run through the house screaming, "Oh, God, I'm sorry! Please forgive me!" I wanted my mother! I wanted things to go back to the way they used to be. I knew that I would do things differently if only I had another chance. I just sat down right in the middle of the kitchen floor, picked up my mother's gown, and wrapped myself up in it. I could still smell her perfume.

I realized I hadn't even eaten since the previous day, and my stomach was making gurgling noises. I grabbed a couple pieces of bread from the bread box and squeezed them tight in my fist and ate them dry. I went to the faucet at the kitchen sink and poured myself a glass of water to wash the bread down. I figured I needed to eat something to (at least) keep up my strength.

I decided to turn on the television again to see what the latest news was and just to figure out what I needed to do at this point; however, I noticed that my eyes felt strange, and they were hard to close when I blinked. I went to the bathroom (near the kitchen) and looked in the mirror to see what was happening with my eyes. I realized that I had cried so bitterly these past couple of days that my eyes were almost swollen shut.

I got a washcloth from the rack and turned on the water faucet. I let the water get warm and drenched the washcloth with the warm water and then wrung it out. I walked over to the sofa, lay down, and placed the cloth over my eyes. I began thinking to myself, *What in the world do I do now?* I kept the towel over my eyes until I dozed off.

Later on, when I woke up, I turned on the news and tried to watch it through my swollen eyes. I listened to all the horror stories of people who were being interviewed; stories of their loved ones disappearing and leaving them behind. Some people were angry while others were repentant. The sad thing about it was that it was a worldwide chaos. Some of the people spoke different languages, but I could feel their pain and agony.

The world news showed footage of disasters all over the world, complete with car pileups on freeways, airplane crashes, pilots missing, and dead bodies everywhere. Babies were missing from nurseries, hospitals, and homes from around the world. Children from other cities who were still in school disappeared from classrooms, and some teachers were missing as well.

I didn't know how I was going to survive. The house felt very cold and empty. I realized that my mother always lit up the room with her humor, her singing, and her personality. I couldn't believe how she used to irritate me, and now, I wish she were here. I just lay there on my sofa until I fell asleep.

CHAPTER 4

THIS WAS NOT GOING TO
BE AN ORDINARY DAY

The next morning, I woke up still lying on the sofa and decided to go out and sit on my porch again to see what was going on outside. I sat there on that hard metal chair for what seemed to be hours looking at all the people passing by. Some of them looked lost while others were walking fast like they were on a mission. I thought to myself, *Where are they going? What mission are they on?*

I kind of snapped out of my stupor, looked at my watch, and realized it was going on three o'clock in the afternoon. I went back into the house to the kitchen to see what I could find to eat. I came to the conclusion that I really wanted to live and that, to do that, I had to keep up my strength. I didn't know what was going to happen next, so I needed to be prepared.

I remembered how my mother would often say, "Just in case you get left behind after the rapture, I have left some instructions to help you find your way to safety in Jesus Christ." I would always laugh and say, "Okay, Mom, whatever!" I didn't want to hear it. She even said she left me a letter in our "big family Bible," but I never had the courage to read it. But this day was different. The words that she said rang out in my mind: "You will find a letter that will help you if you are left behind and enduring the tribulation period."

A cold chill ran over my entire body. I had to come to grips with myself that my worst nightmare had actually come to pass. I was one of those who did not heed the call of God to repent, and now, I was living in the horrors of the tribulation period's unveiling.

I walked over to the coffee table in my living room, picked up the family Bible, and opened it right to the place where my mother left the letter. It smelled like her favorite perfume, and I broke down and cried because it was a memory of her. I held the letter close to my bosom for a few minutes and closed my eyes to try to picture what she looked like and what was going on through her mind when she wrote this letter.

As I began to open the letter, I noticed the pages had smears on them. I thought to myself, *What in the world is this?* It was a light-brown color like water had dropped on some of the pages. Then, it dawned on me, *She was crying when she wrote this. These are her tears that dripped on the pages.* I began to cry as I held the letter (once again) close to my chest as if hugging my mother. I wanted her to know it was all right. She didn't fail me; I failed myself.

I then focused my attention on the letter. I thought to myself, *What warning would be contained in this letter? What horrors will unfold that I will soon have to face? Will I be able to bear it?* It read:

My dear daughter Stacie,

If you find that you have been left behind, and I have been caught up in the rapture, I want you to read this article that I came across the other day written for those who have been left behind. I want you to keep it in a safe place so that you will have instructions on how to survive the tribulation period. Please know that I love you and that I prayed for you that you would turn your life over to God. Please read:

I know right now you are very confused and really don't know what's going on. The only thing you know is that many people (myself included) have simply vanished into thin air. No rationale. No warning. No anything. Just *poof*, we're gone. I have said many times this would happen, just as Jesus Christ promised and the prophets foretold many years before Jesus.

But I, and the others who have been raptured, knew this day was coming, and we were prepared. Many times, I tried to talk to you about this, and I don't think you quite believed me or perhaps just were not ready for the truth. Out of all the countless people missing, we had one thing in common despite our many racial and ethnic differences; we all have accepted Jesus Christ as our Lord and Savior, the Redeemer of all mankind.

There are going to be conspiracy theories as people try to explain what has happened and why so many people simply vanished all at once. Some of the theories may be mass alien abductions, a science experiment gone wrong, mass suicide, etc. None of those are even remotely true, and the fact that you are reading this message is proof of that.

If you are reading this after the rapture, you need to realize that you have been left behind. At this time, you may be feeling rejected by God. You might be saying to yourself, *Why didn't he take me?* or *I don't understand. I wasn't a bad person.* The problem isn't that God rejected you; the problem is that you have rejected him. By not committing your life to Jesus and by declining to follow him, you have left him with no choice but to leave you behind.

I know! I know! There are all sorts of Christians running around now insisting that this explanation *cannot* be the correct one because *they* are left behind. This may include some very visible Christians and respected Christian leaders. What does this tell you? It tells you that any "Christian" left behind was a phony.

I have always said that attending church does not make one saved; any more than sitting in a garage makes a car.

Right now, you may be asking yourself what we did differently. We chose Jesus Christ as our only salvation; however, you chose to ignore him, thinking that you had plenty of time to get saved. Jesus did not want you to be left behind, and the great news is, even though you missed the rapture, he is giving you a second chance, but I'm sorry to say, this second chance comes with a high price. There is about to be a great judgment brought onto the world, and the sinful ways of mankind are about to be punished.

The next few years will be the darkest period in the history of mankind. This is what Christians preached about called the "great tribulation." Do not worry for me or for others who have gone but instead worry about the things that will shortly take place. I want you to stay vigilant against those who seek to do you harm as you have the truth in front of you, and in these dark days ahead, that will make you an enemy of the system.

The article went on to say, "You may ask yourself how I knew this day was coming, and you did not. After all, you considered yourself to be a very intelligent person and that you were too young to give up the pleasures of life as a teenager. But the fact is you were blind because you put your faith in yourself rather than in Jesus Christ.

"You may have thought the rapture would not happen, and it was just a myth. Ever since his defeat at the cross, Lucifer has been biding his time waiting for this moment to deceive even more to take the mark of the beast imposed on all by the Antichrist. And with the true believers of Christ out of the way, Lucifer utilizes his agenda to get back at God."

Mom went on to say:

Trust me, Stacie, it is not too late to give your heart to the Lord. Accept Jesus as your Lord and Savior now!

If you don't know how to pray to God for your salvation, pray this prayer and mean it with all of your heart, mind, and soul:

Lord, I give my entire life to you for your service. I am no longer in control of it, you are. Take my life and lead me along your righteous path. I surrender my total being to you. I shed my old self and ask you to make me a new creation. I repent of all of my sins and ask your forgiveness. I know I am not worthy but because of your loving grace, you sent your Son Jesus to pay the penalty for my sins. He shed his blood on the cross and conquered the grave so that I may have eternal life. I believe in this sacrifice of love and accept the gift of salvation.

Stacie, if you prayed this prayer, you have been set free and born again. Trust God to see you through this terrible time and ask him to give you "holy boldness" so that you will not give in to the evil dictator that will come on the scene. Please know that he is the "Antichrist" and will deceive many by convincing them to take his mark. *Do not take this mark. Do not be deceived.* This mark will seal your fate as a follower of the Antichrist and Satan. God will show you what to do and how to escape.[9]

Please know that I have prayed for you, and I look forward to seeing you with me soon in Glory!

Love, Mom!

After reading the letter from my mom and the article about the rapture, I was numb. I didn't know what to think or how to react. *Wow!* This was real! This was not a joke nor was it a dream. I had really been left behind. I sat on the sofa for what seemed to be several hours reading the letter over and over again to get it locked in my memory. The more I read it, the more afraid I felt, but I also felt a sense of peace come over me. "I still have a chance to give my life to God? I still have a chance?"

I slid down from the sofa, got on my knees, and wept bitterly as I cried out to God to save me. "God, I am so sorry I took your love for granted. I am sorry that I didn't heed the warnings that my mother and Pastor Moore gave me, nor did I embrace the message that Pastor Ray preached. How foolish and stubborn I had been. Please, please forgive me and save me. I accept you into my heart as my Lord and Savior. I confess my sins and want to live for you, Lord! Please help me to face whatever is coming next during this time of tribulation. Give me the strength to be a witness for you to those who have been left behind and will hear your words. In Jesus's name, *amen!*"

At that very moment, I knew God heard my prayer and that I was a new person. I got up from my knees feeling like a new "Stacie."

---

[9] "A Letter to Those Left Behind," City-Data, last modified April 21, 2009, http://www.city-data.com/forum/christianity/627168-letter-those-left-behind.html.
Revelation 13:16–18 (KJV)

For some reason, the dread and fear were not as bad, and I felt that God was going to be with me.

I began to read some of the passages of scripture in the family Bible that my mother had previously bookmarked and highlighted. I felt such a warm feeling in my stomach. I thought to myself, *So this is what my mother always talked about would happen if I gave my heart to the Lord.* I hated the fact that I waited until the rapture took place before I came to my senses; however, my new faith in God was going to get me through this. I was also glad that my mother was with Jesus. If anybody deserved to go to heaven, it was my mother. She was so special to me, even though I didn't tell her that often enough, but she was a good example of what holiness was supposed to be. She lived the life that she talked about by showing me how to be faithful to God and to the church. I remembered how she often shared what she had with some of our neighbors, even though they would talk about her behind her back.

I recall how one day she cooked a big pot of homemade soup and took it across the street to the Robinson family when she found out that the whole family had the flu. Ms. Robinson would hardly even speak to my mom and would turn her head whenever my mom waved at her while working in the yard. Her kids were disrespectful as well; however, my mother found out that they were all sick and ministered to them by taking them that pot of soup.

I remember how I got so mad at her for taking that soup to that family. Her reply to me was "Stacie, honey, one day you will understand why I am reaching out to Ms. Robinson. I am showing her the love of Christ." I guess it worked because a couple of weeks later, I saw my mother wave at Ms. Robinson, and she waved back at her and said, "Thank you so much for all you did for me and my kids."

They even became friends, and my mother invited her to come to church with us. The good part about it was she took my mother up on the offer during the Sunday morning of the revival when Pastor Ray gave that powerful message. I saw Ms. Robinson and her kids make their way to the altar and gave their hearts to the Lord. I was so proud of my mother and the fact that she allowed the Lord to use her to win Ms. Robinson and her children to Christ.

It was also sad because I allowed my fears and my stubbornness to get the best of me, and here I am (now) in this predicament. But thanks be to God, I still have another chance to get it right. I had a newfound faith and strength that God was with me, even though I still had a fear of the unknown.

I had so many questions swirling in my mind: Who will take care of me now? What is going to happen to those of us who have been left behind? Who can I trust? How will I get food? All these things swarmed in my mind.

CHAPTER 5

THE REVEALING
OF PURE EVIL

Weeks have passed, and I have kept a steady routine of waking up, taking my shower, eating breakfast, turning on the TV for the latest news, and reading the passages of scripture in the Bible that my mother had highlighted. I would keep the news channel on all day, maybe go out, and sit on my porch and watch people walking up and down the street looking like zombies with empty stares on their faces.

However, on this particular day, I woke up with a mission on my mind. I needed to figure out how I was going to get food and toiletry items. It had been several weeks since I missed the rapture. My mom had stocked enough food in our pantry so that I was able to stretch it these last few weeks. I used to laugh at my mom for buying everything she could think of that was on sale at the grocery store. I chuckled to myself, *My mother was the coupon queen.* She always caught those two for the price of one bargain on cereal, canned goods, rice, noodles, bread (she had several loaves frozen in our freezer), toothpaste, toilet paper, soap, and spray starch. However, those things really came in handy during these trying times. Even with all of those things I still had in the pantry, I needed meat, milk, juice, eggs, butter, and some toiletries that I ran out of.

I remembered that my mom often told me that she was going to leave some money in her top middle drawer just in case I would need it during this horrible time. I opened the door to her bedroom and began to rummage through the dresser drawers. I felt something hard in the middle drawer underneath all of her sweaters. It was an old wooden box with a tan coarse-looking string tied around it. I got a pair of scissors from the top drawer and cut the string on the box so that I could open it. When I pried the lid open, there were several denominations of bills in it. There were twenties, tens, and several single-dollar bills. I counted about $1,500 in all. I thought to myself, *Wow! This will last quite a while.*

I took one of the twenty-dollar bills out of the wooden box and put it in my pants pocket. I tied the box back up and placed it under my mom's sweaters. I got my front door key off of the hook in the kitchen, put on my jacket, and walked out on the front porch. I locked the door behind me and bolted down the steps and headed to the neighborhood party store. I felt like I was on a mission. I needed to be brave and confident. I didn't make a list, so I rehearsed over and over in my mind what I needed to purchase. *I need meat, milk, bread, eggs, juice, and toiletry items.*

The store was about five or six blocks from my house, but I didn't mind the walk. Even though it was late in the afternoon, it was still daylight, and I didn't feel too afraid. *I hadn't been out of the house in a very long time, except for sitting on the porch, so this was good for me,* I thought.

As I walked down the street toward the store, I noticed that people were looking at me so strange and had a mean countenance on their faces. *What is wrong with these people?* I thought to myself. They wouldn't even respond when I said *hello.* Some of them even purposely bumped into me as though they were secretly hoping I would retaliate so they could get into a fight. I just kept my head down, praying that I would be all right, and started picking up my pace as I walked.

When I finally made it to "Mr. Chen's Market," I saw something so horrific that I froze on my feet for a minute. It was total chaos going on. A mob of people had broken out the large front display window of the store, and people were climbing through the broken glass and looting everything from the shelves. I couldn't believe what was happening. Mr. and Mrs. Chen were such a nice old Asian couple, and they would often let people get away without paying for their groceries if they said they didn't have any money and allow them to pay later. I thought to myself, *They did not deserve this!*

Poor Mr. Chen was lying on the floor, covered in flour, and blood running down his forehead. His glasses were broken and sitting sideways on his face. He was screaming in his broken English, "Please, people! Please, people! Don't steal my store! Don't steal my store!" Mrs. Chen was lying on the floor with her head in Mr. Chen's lap, covered with blood and broken glass. I didn't know if she were dead or alive.

People were stepping all over them and grabbing everything they could get from the shelves. I looked around to see what I could find, but everything I needed was just about gone or busted. However, I did see a carton of milk lying on the floor that hadn't been opened, a bag of sugar that was slightly busted open, a bag of potato chips, and a carton of eggs with only a few in it that were not broken. I hurried up and grabbed those items and noticed a small bright yellow box that had been kicked under the front counter. It was a box of butter, so I reached down and grabbed it before someone else did.

There was so much chaos going on that I didn't know who to give my money to pay for the food items, so I found a couple of plastic bags at the end of the counter, stuffed the items in the bag, and just took off running out of that store. I was in shock and so terrified that I might have gotten seriously hurt. It was like something I saw on television with the "zombies" looting the city.

I bolted out of that store with my bag tucked under my jacket so no one would try to snatch it from me. I started running down the street and praying underneath my breath, "Lord, please protect me! Lord, please protect me!"

All of a sudden, I saw a mob running down the street toward me with clubs and chains in their hands. I didn't know if they were after me or someone else. I spotted an old-abandoned storefront ahead of me on the corner that had been closed and boarded up for years,

so I ran as fast as I could and ducked in the doorway of that building. It reeked of urine and alcohol. The smell was so bad that my
eyes burned, and I had to cover my nose. I felt as though I would
vomit from the smell; however, I was relieved when the mob ran
right past me. As they passed, I saw people running behind them
carrying whole sofas, lamps, and flat-screen televisions that they had
stolen from the nearby furniture store. I was in total shock. I thought
to myself, *These people are insane.*

After they passed, I made sure there was quite a distance between
me and them before I attempted to make it home. I ducked out from
the abandoned building and took off running toward my house as
fast as I could. Those were the longest six blocks I had ever experienced. It seemed like I was running forever. My legs felt like weights.
Everything was moving in slow motion.

When I finally got to my front porch, I felt as though I was
going to faint from exhaustion and fear; however, I managed to make
it up to my front porch steps and to the front door. I reached in my
jacket pocket for my keys and began to fumble, trying to get them
out of my pocket; the keys fell down on the porch and almost went
down the crack. I bent down and picked them up looking around
to see if that mob had caught up with me. My hands were shaking
badly, and my breathing was labored. I scooped up the keys, and after
several attempts, I finally got the door open and (literally) fell onto
the floor in the foyer. I began to cry and thanked God that I didn't
get hurt. *What an experience!*

It seemed as though the whole world had gone mad ever since
the rapture took place. There was an evil presence in the air that was
taking over. People were oblivious to what was happening and had
gone into survival mode. It reminded me of a documentary my mom
and I watched when she was still here. It was about this militia group
who believed they were the only righteous ones left on planet earth
and were living out in the woods, trying to survive on food rations
and waiting for their Messiah to take them to another planet. They
looked so desperate and scared, especially their children. The other
people, not in the group, formed mobs and began to go crazy and
looted other people for food and other provisions. This was the same

look many of the people I saw passing through the streets had on their faces.

I put the grocery items in the refrigerator and in the kitchen cabinets and just stood there for several minutes, trying to catch my breath and calm myself down. I (then) walked into the living room and plopped down on the sofa totally exhausted and turned on the news to find out the latest events that were unfolding.

When the newscaster came on, he began to disclose something so horrific. It made me sit straight up.

"Breaking news! We have just been informed that the recent disappearance of thousands of people from the earth has been proven to be an actual alien/UFO phenomenon and not the previous speculation that God took all of the righteous people away. Let's hear a special message from Dr. Benetue Commeme."

The man who was introduced looked very tall and quite handsome. He had an olive-colored skin tone and a slight accent with the prettiest black hair. I thought to myself, *Who in the world is this guy?* I knew that (lately) most of the news commentators constantly talked about a man who had mysteriously come into power during this chaotic time and began to bring calm and peace to the world. I thought to myself, *How can someone who was pretty much unknown just rise into power so quickly? Could he be the Antichrist?*

As he walked over to the microphone, there was a hush and a look of respect on the faces of the news commentators. He began to speak with an intriguing accent:

"Ladies and gentlemen, I want to (first) praise all of the brilliant men and women who created the technology that allows me to speak to people all over the world. The higher power of the universe has given them the wisdom to create unimaginable things. Trust me, this is only the beginning. You are going to see some pretty amazing things from my administration. I have been chosen to lead and take care of you.

"I know you have many questions, and many of you are hurting and are scared because of the recent event that took place a couple of months ago. I am here to reassure you that all will be well. Please, do not be afraid!

"Many of you who are listening to me now are suffering because your loved ones were in that group of people who supposedly 'vanished' into thin air. And you have been deeply troubled due to a lie that some of our poor, misguided religious leaders had you believe that one day, they would be taken out of this world in an event called the 'rapture' by some entity they called Jesus Christ and that those who did not believe would be left behind. Well, this is absurd!

"There are millions of good people all over this world who are still here that are upstanding citizens in their communities. These people are from different ethnic groups, backgrounds, and from different faiths. You see, it doesn't matter what religion you are as long as you are true to your beliefs. This higher power is all love and would never take certain people away and leave the rest of us here.

"The government has confirmed to me (with proof) that this phenomenon that took place was not the rapture of Christians but an alien attack on our planet earth. People all over the world have been taken by aliens for unknown reasons. These aliens have been on the world government radar for some time; however, we didn't know what they were up to until they took millions of our people away.

"Ladies and gentlemen, this is a serious time right now. We don't know what's coming next, so we are asking you to please be cautious and stay close to your homes until we can figure out what these aliens want. We will update you as more details come in. Remember, I am your leader! I have been chosen to lead you to 'peace.' Leaders all over the world have given me their blessings and have signed over their allegiance and governance to me to lead the world into 'utopia and prosperity!' You can trust me! You can trust me! Do not be afraid!"

I could not believe my eyes and my ears! At that moment, I remembered what Pastor Ray said would happen. He said, "Based on 2 Thessalonians 2:5–13, it clearly states that after the rapture of the church, Satan will unleash his deception or 'lie' on a worldwide scale to the point that he will explain away the rapture—in part by way of an 'alien' disclosure and direct contact.

"After the rapture takes place, there will be a great shock around the world. People will be so devastated. A mysterious leader will rise, and all of the world leaders will (readily) believe in a great deception. He will disclose that the thousands of born-again believers who simply vanished from the face of the earth were really abducted by a UFO.[10]" Now, I was actually hearing the lie and seeing it unfold firsthand.

After his startling message, I recalled that my mother said she left many articles and sermons in our family Bible to read just in case I missed the rapture. I picked up the family Bible from the coffee table and found the scripture she had highlighted in *2 Thessalonians 2:9–12 (KJV):*

> The coming of the lawless one is according to the working of Satan, with all power, signs, and lying wonders, and with all unrighteous deception among those who perish, because they did not receive the love of the truth, that they might be saved. And for this reason God will send them strong delusion that they should believe the lie that they all may be condemned who did not believe the truth but had pleasure in unrighteousness.

---

[10] "UFOs Explaining Away the Rapture?" Rapture Forums, published July 30, 2020, https://www.raptureforums.com/end-times/ufos-explaining-away-the-rapture.

CHAPTER 6

A GOD-GIVEN FRIENDSHIP

Day after day, I kept a steady routine of waking up in the morning, showering and getting dressed, eating breakfast, watching the latest news, eating lunch, preparing dinner, and reading the Bible. This routine was quite satisfying for me as God was revealing himself to me more and more.

I was no longer afraid, and I even found a way of rationing the food that my mom had stored away in the food pantry. I just had to figure out how to get more dairy products. I still had plenty of money in the box that was in Mom's drawer, but Mr. Chen's store was closed because it had been completely looted.

One morning, there was a knock on my door. I thought to myself, *Who in the world is this? I am not answering that door! It could be that mob or someone trying to rob me.* I got up from the sofa and went to my front door and peeked out of the small triangular window. To my surprise, it was my neighbor Mr. Anthony Lewis knocking at the door. *What in the world does he want?* I thought to myself. *He was in such bad shape the last time I saw him on the day of the rapture when his wife and son disappeared.*

I cracked open the door (slightly) and replied, "Yes, can I help you?" He replied, "I'm just checking on you to see if you are all right. I know you are by yourself, and you were so nice to check on me the day my wife and son disappeared. You don't have to be afraid. I just wanted to make sure you were all right."

For some reason, I didn't feel afraid of him, and I felt as though God was sending me someone who would look out for me. I opened the door and invited him in. All my logical senses were telling me it was dangerous to let this man in my house, but at the same time, I sensed a peace that it was okay. I said, "Come on in and have a seat."

When he came in, I noticed how thin and disheveled he looked. He sat down on the living room sofa and kept looking at my peanut butter and jelly sandwich that was sitting on the coffee table that I had made for lunch. I realized that he probably was hungry, so I asked him if he wanted me to fix him a sandwich as well. He was so polite and refused it at first. I finally convinced him to let me fix him a sandwich.

After I fixed him a sandwich, I placed the saucer on the table in front of him along with a cold glass of water. Mr. Lewis grabbed that sandwich and gobbled it up so fast. It seemed like he only took two or three bites, and it was gone. We looked at each other, and both of us began to laugh so hard. I teased him and said, "Mr. Lewis, you looked like a caveman in a cartoon that I used to watch on TV. Are you sure you still have your fingers? Or did you eat them too?" That made us laugh even harder. He asked for seconds, and I made him another sandwich.

The TV was on my usual news channel so that I could keep up with all the events that were unfolding. Suddenly, the newscaster caught our attention and announced that our new world leader, Dr. Benetue Commeme, was about to come on the air with another message. Mr. Lewis asked me if I minded if he stayed and watched the news with me. I gladly obliged because I needed the companionship, and so did he.

As Dr. Benetue Commeme began to speak, I noticed that Mr. Lewis was frowning at what he was saying. I asked him if he believed the words that the man was saying, and he said, "Are you kidding me? That man is looney tunes." I was so glad to hear him say that because it opened up a door for me to witness to him and to lead him to accept Jesus Christ into his life.

We continued watching the message from Commeme and the lies he was giving to the people. We talked for hours as I shared with him what happened to me that Sunday night when Pastor Ray preached that powerful message and how I refused to give my heart to the Lord. I showed him the passages in the Bible that my mom had highlighted and the letter that she left me about the rapture.

This was the beginning of a great friendship, and we both looked forward to spending time together. He became like a father to me. I was too little to understand what happened when my own father died when I was only three. I just remembered missing him when I saw pictures of him in my mom's bedroom and on her dresser, and she would share stories of how he used to carry me on his shoulders and put me to bed at night.

CHAPTER 7

IT'S TIME TO MAKE
A DECISION

Mr. Lewis began to come over to my house every day for lunch, then we would prepare dinner together, and afterwards have bible study. He became quite a Bible scholar and would even explain some of the words and meanings in the Bible that I didn't understand.

We had a daily routine of eating lunch and dinner together and watching the worldwide news channel and Bible study. He became more and more like my father, and I think he felt as though I was like a daughter to him. I thanked God for bringing him into my life because I had someone to share this journey with. He even shared with me some of the food he had at his house, and we found another store we could go to, and we each shared our finances.

One particular day, as we were preparing dinner, I turned on the news. The new world leader, Dr. Benetue Commeme, came on the air and made an announcement that changed the world as we knew it. He began to explain how he had put together a team of super guards who were going to set up and operate local stations throughout the entire world to carry out his new plan and to step up security. These guards would be responsible for making sure that every person throughout the world would make a pledge to give their allegiance to him and to the New World Organization. He went on to say:

"My scientists have created an unbelievable program that I am so excited about. I am going to use this program to monitor every person in the world and make sure they are safe. I will be requiring every one of you, under the sound of my voice, to report to one of the stations that I have set up in every city, state, and country around the world. You will have six weeks to register. You will be given a mark on your forehead or your hand. Don't worry about the rumors you may hear. It is not some sort of mind control like those people who vanished had you to believe. It is painless, and it will only be visible under ultraviolet rays. It is a sophisticated system set up so that you will be able to purchase food, clothes, and to do trade if you are a business owner.

"As you know, I told you that we were going to institute a new money system. We will no longer need to use currency because it is so outdated. With this new system, people will no longer be able to fraudulently steal or hack your credit cards or steal your identity. This new system can detect all fraudulent activity.

"This mark will have a computer chip in it, which will contain all of your banking and financial information, your social security number, and all of your pertinent information. So instead of receiving cash, paychecks, welfare, EBT cards, alimony, or any finances you have earned will be recorded right on that computer chip, which is connected to our new supercomputer.[11]

"Just think about it! No more worrisome trips to the bank or credit unions or waiting for the mailman to bring your paycheck. Once you receive this computer chip implanted under your skin, when you go to the grocery store or try to purchase anything, you will be scanned by trained men and women who work for our New World Organization called 'One Way United.' They have been ordered to make sure you have our computer chip inserted. This

---

[11] Revelation 13:16–18 (KJV)
   "Does a cashless society have anything to do with the end times?" Got Questions, ww.gotquestions.org/cashless-society.html.

process is being implemented all over the world as I speak. You will recognize our special guards because they will have the organization's name on their uniforms. Remember the name One Way United.

"So I am giving you fair warning. Every man, woman, boy, and girl is required to receive this chip. This process is very important to maintain peace and order. If you do not receive it, you will be arrested.

"This is all I have to report to you this evening. Remember, I am your leader! Let me take away all of your cares and burdens. You don't have to fear because I love you! I am here to help each and every one of you to experience 'Shalom,' which means peace, safety, and prosperity."

After he finished his speech, the two newscasters came back on the air. It was a man and a woman. The man spoke and said, "Well, people, you heard it from the man himself. I guess I will be heading to one of our local stations in my neighborhood to get registered tomorrow." He looked over at the female commentator and said, "What about you? Are you going to get this implanted chip?" She answered and said, "Are you kidding me? Of course! Listen! I like to eat, and I like shopping. These are modern times with new technology, and we have to go with the flow."

Mr. Lewis and I could not believe what we just heard. He looked at me for the first time with fear and dread. I felt so overwhelmed, stunned, and scared. It was really happening, just like the Bible said. Dr. Benetue Commeme actually revealed himself to those of us who knew the truth as the Antichrist. We were actually watching it unfold right before our eyes.

At that very moment, a spirit of prayer came over us. We both got down on our knees and wept bitterly as we prayed for strength to resist this evil man's plan and for God's protection for the things that were about to take place.

CHAPTER 8

IT'S TIME TO TAKE A STAND

Months have passed since I wrote in my journal; however, my faith has gotten stronger and stronger. Mr. Lewis and I have been staying strong keeping up our Bible study and spending time together as father and daughter. I was so glad God sent this gentleman in my life, and he always told me that he was so glad to have me as the daughter he never had.

It's funny how God knew I was going to go through the tribulation period and that I was too young to live by myself without a parent figure to guide me. I know the bond between Mr. Lewis and I was God-ordained. My mom is probably looking down and is happy that I have someone looking out for me during these trying times.

Mr. Lewis decided to move into my house permanently. We had become more and more like father and daughter, and we spent most of our days together eating meals, Bible study, and watching the latest news. Things had started getting very dangerous for a young girl to be living by herself. The mobs and looters became more and more violent. They started breaking into houses and stealing anything they could get their hands on, so it was not good for me to be by myself.

He also said it was too painful, and he had too many memories of his wife and son to stay (alone) at his house. So one day, he just packed up most of his clothes and essentials from his house along with some meat and nonperishable food items (mostly canned goods) from his cupboard that he thought we could use. He boarded up all of his windows and put chains and locks on his doors. He also brought his wife's Bible with him because he diligently studied it, especially the things she had highlighted. He even found a notebook with all of her written notes and different subjects she had been studying, which were fascinating to him. He told me that he felt so foolish because he didn't listen to her when she witnessed to him and begged him to go to church with her. We both were so thankful that, according to the Bible, we still had a chance.

Today was a very important and unusual day. I woke up hearing the birds chirping in my backyard tree, and the sun was shining so bright. You wouldn't think we were living in the tribulation period because it was such a beautiful day. I got up and continued my usual routine; taking my shower, getting dressed, and going downstairs to cook breakfast. Mr. Lewis (who is now sleeping in our guest bedroom) would usually get up, get dressed, and join me in the kitchen to help prepare breakfast.

While he was making the grits, I went into the living room to turn on the news (as always); however, the words "breaking news" began flashing in a box below the TV screen. All of a sudden, the face of Dr. Benetue Commeme came on the screen, and he began to say something that would change the world as we knew it:

"Greetings, ladies and gentlemen, I bring you peace and love as an ambassador of the power of the universe. This message is to all people and to all nations around the world. If you recall, I put out a mandate several weeks ago for everyone to go to their local 'One World United' registration stations that have been set up to make it easier for you to register and to receive the much-needed computer chip implant. We are going to call it my 'mark.' We have created a computer system that has the capacity to store all pertinent information of every person in the entire world. It will also have the ability to administer the computer chip. We call this computer system the 'beast' because it is so powerful, and no one has ever seen anything like it. So we want everyone under the sound of my voice to register and take the 'mark of the beast' as soon as possible.

"To make it easier for you, I am sending out my 'special guards' from the One Way United bureau to every city, state, and country to ensure that this task is implemented. Within the next couple of weeks, they will be dispatched to go door to door to make sure everyone has gone to their local station and received this mark. If not, they will provide you with transportation to your local station to accomplish my goal of making sure everyone will be registered so you will be able to buy food, shop, go to the doctor, and live normal lives.

"Now, let me give you fair warning! Those of you who refuse to take this mark of the *beast* will be arrested on the spot and placed in deprogramming camps that we have already set up until you make a decision to comply. This has to be done in order to keep law and order around the world.

"I am sure all of you want what's best for all of us. Remember, we are now One Way United! Shalom! Shalom! I send blessings to each and every one of you from the universal power that rules this world."

Mr. Lewis and I were shocked and devastated! We only had a couple of weeks to decide what we were going to do. Just recently, we realized that our food supplies were running low, and we needed to get more groceries. It was dangerous to venture out of the house because of all of the mobs and looters roaming the neighborhoods. Now, the Antichrist's henchmen were going to be searching the homes of everyone to see if we had gotten the mark of the *beast*.

We sat down at the table, held hands, and prayed for strength and guidance as we ate the breakfast we had prepared. We also got out our Bibles and started our Bible study for the day. Mr. Lewis read a scripture from Isaiah 41:10, "Fear not, for I am with you; be not dismayed, for I am your God; I will strengthen you, I will help you, I will uphold you with my righteous right hand." We discussed how God wanted us to trust him and not to be afraid because he will be with us. He was going to strengthen us and help us in every situation we found ourselves in. He said he would hold us with his "righteous hand." After our Bible study, we cleaned up the breakfast dishes and continued to watch the world news channel. I pulled out my journal to write more about the things I had been going through since that dreadful day when my mom and all of the Christians were taken out of this world to be with the Lord. Mr. Lewis sat next to me reading more scriptures and taking notes.

All of a sudden, Mr. Lewis (finally) broke the silence and announced that he had an idea. He said, "How about me going down the street to my house, get my car out of my garage, and drive around town to see what grocery stores are open for business without the presence of Dr. Benetue Commeme's henchmen. According to him, we still have a couple of weeks before they come after us. So that will be our adventure for today." I agreed, and he followed with "Let's pray for God's safety and protection as we venture out." I never thought I would be such a devout prayer warrior, but I found out the importance of prayer.

We got down on our knees, and Mr. Lewis earnestly prayed, "Dear Lord! We are in your care. Please protect us from this man of perdition and his guards. Lord, please protect us and all of those who will refuse to take this mark. Show us your will and give us direction. We trust you, Lord! We trust you, Lord! Amen!"

I decided to dry the dishes and put them back in the cabinet while Mr. Lewis took a chance to walk down the street to his house and get his car out of the garage. It seemed like hours before he returned. I was so nervous that I kept looking out of my window to see if the mob had stopped him and robbed him.

He finally drove up in my driveway and honked the horn for me to come out of the house. I hurriedly went into my mom's bedroom and got some money out of her middle drawer. Something in my spirit told me to take all of it with us, so I grabbed all of the money, got my jacket from the front closet, rolled up the money, and put it in my pocket. I then got the house keys from the hook in the kitchen and (nervously) walked outside on the porch. I locked the door behind me, looked around to see if it was safe, and made a mad dash to Mr. Lewis's car.

When I got in the car, I could tell that Mr. Lewis was very nervous. He said, "Honey, this is going to be a test of our faith. Are you up for the challenge?" I answered, "God is going to be with us, I can feel it. I don't know why, but something spoke to me and told me to take all of the money from the box in my mom's drawer." I pulled out the money and gave it to him. He said, "Well, God will reveal it to us." We held hands and prayed one more time, and then we pulled off, not knowing what to expect.

As we were driving, we noticed people walking up and down the streets with blank stares on their faces. They almost looked like robots. We began to drive around several blocks checking out different grocery stores to see if they were open.

As we rounded one corner, we began to see "One World United" trucks parked in front of a couple of the stores, so we knew not to stop there. We were shocked that they had already begun setting up the registration stations in our little town. We continued to drive around searching, which seemed like forever, until we finally came upon the "Crescent Grocery Store" that had an Open for Business sign in the front window. We didn't see any of the special guards in front, so we decided to take a chance and go to that store.

There was a sweet Black couple standing at the door and greeted us as we walked in. They indicated that they didn't have much, but we were welcomed to purchase whatever we could find. We grabbed one of the shopping carts that were in the front of the store. As we walked around the store, checking out every aisle for nonperishable canned goods and some dairy products, I noticed that the couple kept staring at us. I thought to myself, *Why are they looking at us? It was freaking me out.* I mentioned it to Mr. Lewis, and he said he noticed it too. So we grabbed as many canned goods as we could, and I got some bread, peanut butter, jelly, milk, orange juice, and eggs, and we walked to the front counter to pay.

The lady rang up our groceries while her husband bagged them up. He looked at his wife and nodded at her for some reason. She nodded back at him and reached under the counter for something. It startled me and Mr. Lewis because we didn't know if they had a gun or were signaling for someone to come get us. We were so scared; however, what she picked up was a little booklet from underneath the counter and placed it in one of our bags. She rang up $25.00, which we knew was not the right price. Our groceries had to cost more than that, but they wouldn't take anything more.

Then, the lady's husband looked around acting as if someone might have been watching us and whispered, "When you get in your car, read the booklet. God bless you!" Those words "God bless you" rang out in my ears like a whisper from God himself. Mr. Lewis pulled out $25.00 dollars from the roll of money I had given him and gave it to the friendly lady, thanking her several times. As we grabbed up the grocery bags and started walking toward the door, the woman grabbed my arm and said, "Don't forget to read the booklet that I placed in your bag. God be with you both!"

Mr. Lewis and I said our goodbyes to the couple and walked out of the store to the car feeling a sense of relief. After we put the groceries in the trunk of the car and got in, we prayed and thanked God for protection and favor.

As Mr. Lewis began to drive, I remembered that the couple in the store told us to read the little booklet they had placed in our bag. We pulled over and parked the car so we could get the booklet out of the grocery bag in the trunk. Mr. Lewis popped open the trunk and told me to wait as he looked around to make sure we were safe. He gave the signal to go ahead, and I dashed around the car to the open trunk. I fished through the bags and remembered the little booklet was in the bag with the milk. I retrieved the booklet and slammed the trunk shut and got back in the car.

When we looked at the little booklet, we realized that it was a religious tract about the gift of salvation. We were very curious as to why the couple insisted that we read it; we figured they were Christians and were trying to witness to us. Then we noticed that at the end of the tract, there was a handwritten note taped inside of the back cover. The note read, "After you read this tract, if you believe it, do not take the mark of the *beast*! It is Satan's mark. *We can help you! 'God is our refuge and strength, a very present help in trouble'* (Psalm 46:1). If you need help, please contact us: (311) 555-0121."

Mr. Lewis and I looked at each other wondering what in the world this message meant. We knew that Dr. Benetue Commeme was definitely the Antichrist and that we had been trying to figure out a way to refuse to take the mark of the *beast*. Was this our way out? Was this God sending us help?

As we drove off, I kept reading that message over and over again. After I almost memorized the message, I tucked the tract back in my jacket pocket and laid my head back on the seat headrest and just closed my eyes in exhaustion but also with a sense of relief.

The store was only a half an hour from our house, but as we headed back home, it seemed like it took forever. When we finally started approaching our block, we were in total shock. There were several black vans with flashing lights parked at both ends of the block and men in black carrying strange-looking guns were patrolling the block. Fear gripped my heart as I thought to myself, *What in the world is going on?* I was hysterically shouting to the top of my lungs, "Mr. Lewis, what is going on? Who are those men in uniforms? What are they doing?"

Mr. Lewis motioned for me to be quiet, and he said, "Duck down on the floor!" He slowly turned the car around and drove down to the previous block where there were no black cars at that time. He parked the car at the corner very slowly as not to be noticed. He then ducked down on the floor with me and said, "Stacie, you do believe that God has been protecting us so far, right?" I nodded and answered *yes* with my voice trembling and tears running down my face. He said, "Well, we are in a situation where we are going to have to rely on our faith one more time. Those men in black are the Antichrist's henchmen. They are looking for those of us who don't have the mark of the *beast.* Remember, he made the announcement that he was going to send his men to every neighborhood around the world to make sure they all had the mark. Those who didn't were going to be rounded up and taken to the local deprogramming centers. If anyone refused, they would be arrested. I thought he said he was giving everybody two weeks to get it done, but he deceived us and is carrying out his mandate now."

We stayed down on the floor of the car until Mr. Lewis stood up just enough to peek out of the window. He saw the "One Way United" guards putting some of the people in our neighborhood in their black vans. Some of them were in handcuffs. We knew it wasn't safe to go down our block to our house, so we stayed parked down the street and remained on the floor. We held hands and prayed for God's protection and his direction.

When we finally saw the black vans drive off, Mr. Lewis got up from the floor and peaked out of the window to make sure the coast was clear. He said, "You can get up now, honey! I think we are safe!" He slowly started up the car and drove down to our block.

As we approached our house, we noticed it was all boarded up with signs plastered on the windows and doors. It read, "Property of One Way United." We looked around and noticed that many of our neighbors' houses had the same signs on their windows as well. I asked Mr. Lewis, "What is going on? Did they just take over all of our houses? He answered, "Stacey, I believe they just did." He pointed to his house as well, and we saw the same notice on his windows and doors.

It finally sunk in that we were never going to be able to go back to our homes again. *What are we going to do? Where will we go?* These thoughts flooded my mind, and I was sure Mr. Lewis was thinking the same thing. We just sat there in the car in disbelief about what had just happened. I asked Mr. Lewis if he had any suggestions as to what we were going to do. At first, it seemed as though he was in a trance. He wouldn't answer me; he just held on to the steering wheel very tightly and starred out the window.

He finally spoke and said, "Stacey, give me that tract that couple at the grocery gave us. I believe God has given us a way out. We are going to take a chance and call them and see if they can help us. Let's say a prayer for protection." We held hands and prayed that God would protect us.

I pulled the tract out of my pocket and gave it to Mr. Lewis. He took his cell phone from his pants pocket, took a deep breath, and dialed the number on the handwritten note that was on the back of the tract. After several rings, someone answered the phone and said, "What is your dilemma? How can we help you?" Mr. Lewis began to tell the person on the phone how we got their number from this couple at Crescent Grocery Store. The man on the phone spoke and said, "Did you feel safe and comfortable around the couple in the store? Are you a believer? At first, we were afraid to say yes because we weren't sure whether or not we were walking into a trap.

The man on the phone tried to reassure us that we were safe to answer and to reveal to them that we were believers. He then said, "Hold on a minute! I am going to put someone on the phone." The person that came on the phone was the voice of the friendly owner of Crescent Grocery Store himself. We felt as though weights were lifted off of our shoulders. He reassured us that we were safe to talk on the phone, so we began to share what had just happened to us and that we had nowhere to go and didn't know what to do.

He told us that he and his wife were part of a group of believers who also missed the rapture but gave their hearts to the Lord. He told us that they had been helping people who didn't want to take the mark of the *beast* and were no longer safe in their homes.

He said, "This evening, our store was taken over by the 'One Way United' guards as well. They said they were ordered to take over our store to transform it into a registration station. They gave us until the end of the week to register ourselves, but after they left, we packed up as much as we could in our truck and said farewell to our store. We own some property out in the woods by this beautiful lake. My wife and I often go there for vacations. We figured this would be a perfect spot to hide out and be a refuge for people who, like us, needed shelter from this new world leader and his guards.

"If you feel safe with me and my wife, I want you to join this group of believers. We are a small group of believers who have refused to take the mark of the *beast*. We come from all walks of life and have been hiding in this obscure place that (for now) has not been detected. We have stored up plenty of food, and we have plenty of beds to accommodate you."

Mr. Lewis and I looked at each other and realized that this was God giving us a way of escape. This was going to be our new home. Mr. Lewis asked the man his name, and he told us his name was William, but everybody called him "Brother Willie." He said his wife's name was Sister Betty. Mr. Lewis then asked Brother Willie how we would find this place of safety. Brother Willie told us to give him our location, and he would send someone to find us and lead us to where they were. We gave him our location, and he instructed us to wait for someone to come and get us.

We sat in our car for quite a while, and as we waited, we saw several cars driving down the street. Some of them even slowed down and glanced inside our car as if they were wondering what we were doing just sitting there. It was very scary, but we knew God was protecting us. We prayed for strength to face this next chapter in our lives because we didn't know what to expect. We just knew that we were in the hands of Almighty God. I closed my eyes and began to envision what kind of place we were going to. I pondered in my mind, *Was it an old, abandoned building? Was it a cave out in a wooded area? Or was it a hidden mansion somewhere?*

As we sat in the car, I noticed that it started getting dark outside. The sun was going down. I glanced at the clock on the car dashboard, and it was 6:15 p.m. I was hungry, scared, and didn't know what to expect. I knew that this was another test of our faith in God for protection.

Finally, a royal blue car pulled up alongside of us. The man inside rolled down his window and motioned for us to roll down our window. When we rolled down the window, he asked us our names, and Mr. Lewis said, "I am John Lewis, and this is my daughter, Stacie." I (kind of) smiled because that was the first time he actually called me his daughter. We had developed a father-daughter relationship, but we never said it out loud.

The man in the car said, "Pleased to meet you, Mr. Lewis and Stacie. God bless you both! My name is Brother Timothy. Brother Willie sent me to lead you to our location. Follow me!"

Mr. Lewis or, should I say from now on, my "dad" started up the car, and we began to follow Brother Timothy to our new home. We trailed him for quite a while until we took the service drive and onto the freeway. I was a little scared wondering where we were going, but I was also excited about what God was getting ready to do in our lives.

My dad began singing this old hymn that he said his wife used to sing when she was in the car while driving her to the store. I was so happy that I actually had a new dad. I joined in with him as we sang, "Onward, Christian soldiers! Marching as to war with the cross of Jesus going on before!"

CHAPTER 9

MEETING OUR NEW FAMILY

The drive to our new home took about two hours. As we were driving, Dad reached over and opened the glove compartment and pulled out a black leather case. He told me that his wife used to play those tapes all the time. He popped one of them in the CD player and started tapping his fingers to the beat on the steering wheel. It was so funny because he didn't know any of those gospel songs. He told me that he hated it when his wife played those CDs because (secretly) he felt condemned, and he didn't want her to know. So he would demand that she turn on the radio to an R & B station and would tell her he didn't want to hear any of that religious stuff. Now (of course), he wished she was still with him so that the two of them could sing gospel songs together. He told me that he only remembered some of the old hymns he used to sing at his grandmother's church when he was a little boy.

The tapes that his wife had in the car were my kind of gospel music. I couldn't believe she had all of the latest gospel hits that young people liked. I thought to myself, *His wife must have been pretty cool. She probably would have really related to me and my friends from my church.*

We finally got off the freeway and continued to follow Brother Timothy to our new destination. He came upon the service drive, and we trailed close behind so we wouldn't lose him in the traffic and get lost. He drove a little longer until we got to a street that was sort of obscure. If you weren't paying attention, you would miss it. It reminded me of when I spent the summer in Arkansas with my aunt a few years ago. She would drive down these dirt roads that didn't have any streetlights like we did in the city, so it was super dark. I used to wonder how in the world she knew when to turn without running into a ditch, but she always made it to her house that sat tucked in the back away from the main road.

As we followed Brother Timothy down the dark road, it looked like we were in the deep dark woods. Our car began hitting hanging branches, and we began rolling over twigs. I thought to myself, *Where in the world are we going? Where is this place?* My dad didn't say anything, but I could see the look on his face that he was thinking the same thing.

When we (finally) arrived at our destination and pulled up to what looked like a little community of all sizes of tents and trailers, there were people sitting outside of their trailers in lawn chairs, sitting by a fire talking and laughing. It looked like they were quite happy, and I felt a sense of safety. A man came out of one of the tents and motioned for us to pull up in the parking area. As we followed his direction, we stayed in the car and waited to see what else we were supposed to do. I noticed that there were a few kids my age there, boys and girls. Some of them were playing board games, and a couple of the boys were throwing a rubber ball for this cute little brown dog to fetch. However, as I watched them playing, I thought to myself, *This seems strange, there weren't any young children around. Where were the children?* Then I remembered when Pastor Ray mentioned that babies and young children would all be raptured because they were innocent.

Suddenly, a man and a woman came out of their trailer and started walking toward our car. To our surprise, it was Brother Willie and his wife Sister Betty. We were so glad to see their familiar faces. They came to Dad's window and invited us to get out of the car and meet our new family. They began to introduce us to everyone in the camping area close to the parking lot. Sister Betty asked us if we were hungry. Of course, I blurted out right away, "Oh, yes!" Sister Betty gave me a "jovial" laugh and invited us to join her and Brother Willie inside their trailer. As we walked with them toward their trailer, we passed several people who gave us warm nods and greetings of welcome. I grabbed my dad's hand, held it tight, and shook it as a signal to him that we were safe. We both glanced at each other, not speaking a word, but silently, we both took a deep breath of relief, knowing that this was the place God wanted us to be. We told them that we had food in our trunk and that we were willing to share it with the camp members. They told us that they were glad to receive it.

When we arrived at the trailer, we walked up about five steps behind Brother Willie and Sister Betty. They unlocked the door, and we followed them inside. It looked like a very cozy home. I noticed that Sister Betty had a good eye for decorations. Everything was color coordinated with earth-toned colors of beige, brown, and accented with red. Her sofa had quite a few pillows on it, picking up her earth-toned colors. I chuckled to myself reminiscing how my grandmother used to have so many pillows on her sofa that I often wondered where in the world anyone would sit.

Sister Betty motioned for us to have a seat at their kitchen table, and Brother Willie joined. She walked over to the cupboard and got out some bowls, saucers, eating utensils, and glasses. As she sat the items in front of us and walked over to the stove, I noticed that there was a big pot on the stove and a pan of corn bread. She opened the lid and began to stir its contents. A wonderful aroma filled the kitchen. I realized that it was soup, and I couldn't wait to eat some. When it was piping hot, she invited me, my dad, and Brother Willie to bring our bowls over to the stove and get as much soup as we wanted while she cut each of us a piece of corn bread.

Of course, I was the first one to get up, and I dipped the spoon in the large pot. I could tell it was homemade. It was full of potatoes, carrots, big chunks of beef, and other vegetables. After I filled my bowl, I handed my dad the spoon and sat down to eat. I thought to myself, *Now, Stacie, don't embarrass yourself. Wait until the rest of them sits down and you all say the grace.* So I waited for them to dish out their soup and join me at the table. Needless to say, that soup was so good. It reminded me of the soup and corn bread my mom used to make.

We sat at that table and ate the most delicious meal. All of us had seconds as we talked for what seemed to be hours. Brother Willie and Sister Betty shared so much with us about their experience of missing the rapture, and we shared our experiences with them as well. They told us about their new way of life, how living out in the woods came about, and how God directed them to invite others there for shelter.

After we finished eating, Dad and Brother Willie went outside, and I volunteered to help Sister Betty wash the dishes and clean up the kitchen. She was so sweet and "grandmotherly." I had a feeling I was going to really enjoy life in this place.

After we finished washing the dishes, dried them, and put them up in the cabinet, Sister Betty said, "Honey, I have some homemade apple pie in the oven. We can eat some later. Would you like that?" Of course, she didn't have to ask me that question but once. That sounded good to me! I hadn't had homemade pie since my mother was raptured. I answered, "Yes! Yes! Thank you."

We joined Brother Willie and my dad outside after they returned from delivering the groceries and the toiletry items we brought to the main food storage area. We all sat in the folding chairs in front of their trailer and had a nice conversation. Brother Willie asked if we wanted to meet some of the people in the camp, so we followed him around to the different trailers as he introduced us to most of the families who were also sitting outside of their trailers. We felt so welcomed and blessed to be with people who were believers. I met a few teenagers as well, and they looked at me as if they were glad to see someone else their age; however, it still seemed strange that there weren't any babies or little kids there.

Sister Betty said, "Come on, we want you both to meet Pastor Goodman. He is our spiritual leader." We followed the both of them to another trailer, and Sister Betty knocked on the trailer door. The man who appeared at the door was a little short and chubby man with a very pleasant smile. His hair was salt-and-pepper-colored, and he was dressed casually in a green and beige plaid shirt and beige pants. I thought to myself, "This guy looked so familiar to me. I have seen him before, somewhere."

Pastor Goodman came outside and motioned for us to sit down with him in the lawn chairs that were in front of his trailer. We introduced ourselves and him to us. He began to share his testimony with us:

"You know, I used to be a pastor of a prominent church in the city. I loved the Lord with all my heart and started out dedicated to the cause of Christ. However, when I started getting more and more members, our congregation grew to the point that we had to build a bigger place. I began to get caught up with worldly things, and I forgot my spiritual life and about what the role of a pastor should have been. I missed the rapture because of my foolishness, greed, prestige and power. My wife tried to warn me that I was taking the church in the wrong direction, but I wouldn't listen. I went down that dark path of teaching a 'prosperity gospel' to my congregants. I stopped preaching messages of salvation and of lives being changed by the power of God. We ended up becoming a 'megachurch' because I preached what people wanted to hear instead of what they needed.

"A couple of days before the rapture, God had given me a message to preach about deliverance from sin. I pondered over it and even wrote out the sermon under conviction of how my own life had spiraled out of the will of God. However, I began to think that, if I preached that message, it might offend some of my members. They were good tithe payers and gave large offerings, so I put the first message aside and wrote another one that would cater to my members, and (quite frankly), I wanted to keep them coming.

"I can remember the day so vividly. After I preached the watered-down message, my wife looked at me in disgust, and I tried to play it off and not look at her, but that glare she gave me sent a chill down my spine. I knew I had sold out to the enemy and that I didn't preach what God had given me.

"After church services ended, I announced in the microphone not to forget to come back to our evening service. We were going to have a musical. Everybody clapped their hands with excitement, and then we were dismissed. I did my usual hand shaking of those who came up to the pulpit to greet me and my wife. I tried to forget what was really swirling around in my head. God was speaking to me, and I felt so convicted for not preaching what he had given me.

"I went to my office, took off my clergy robe, and hung it up in my closet. I felt a strong urge to fall on my knees and repent, but my pride got in the way, and I put my Bible and notes on my desk and turned on the radio to drown out my thoughts. Normally, after service, I, my wife, and our precious little boy and girl would go out for dinner at one of the local restaurants, and some of the members would join us. So when I walked out of my office, I saw my wife greeting some of the members and told them to meet us at the Ocean Breeze Seafood restaurant. I was glad because they would keep my mind off of that tugging in my heart.

"The ride to the restaurant was very quiet. I didn't know what to say to my wife, and she wouldn't look at me or say anything either. Finally, she broke her silence and said, 'Honey, what are we doing? What has happened to our church? You are taking us in the wrong direction, and I don't like it. As a matter of fact, God doesn't like it. We have left our first love, and I don't know what kind of church we are.' I just replied to her that I didn't want to argue with her and we would table the discussion for when we got home.

"When we arrived at the restaurant, several of the members were already there, and we joined them at the table they had reserved. I was so delighted to see them because they kept my mind off of my thoughts, and my wife cheered up a little bit. We ate, laughed, and really enjoyed the fellowship. After a couple of hours, it was time to go back to church for the gospel concert, and I reminded the members to come back to church for the program.

"When we got back to church, the auditorium had started to get full. I was glad that we had a good turnout for the gospel concert. Our musician had asked me if he could invite this group to be our featured guest. He told me that they were awesome, so I gave him my blessings and trusted his judgment.

"When the program started, the gospel group came on stage with fervor and spiritual energy. I could tell that those young men and women were anointed as they began to usher in the presence of

God. They began to engage the congregation into worshipping the Lord with them. Most of the congregation joined in with them in authentic worship. They looked like they had been starving for the true presence of the Lord. I felt a little guilty because we used to have this type of service years ago, but I turned our services into more of a formal type of worship when dignitaries and high-class people started joining our church. I didn't want to offend them with a jubilant type of worship.

"While I was sitting in the audience next to my wife and my two kids, I glanced at her and noticed that her hands were lifted up to the Lord and tears running down her face in ecstasy. As the gospel group began to sing another song, all of a sudden, they just vanished! *Poof!* They were gone! The clothes that they were wearing just fell off on the stage, and their guitars dropped to the floor, which made their speakers make loud ringing noises. I looked over at my wife and realized she had vanished. All I saw were her clothes in her seat along with my two kids' clothes. I looked around in shock and noticed that quite a few of my church members vanished as well. I stood straight up out of my seat, not knowing what to do or say.

"Some of the members, still in the audience, started screaming and crying hysterically. I was so devastated when I realized what had just happened. The rapture of the church had taken place, and we had been left behind. I tried to console my members, but they were screaming and crying with terror on their faces. Some of them just got up and ran out of the church in total hysteria. I could not believe what had just taken place. My heart was racing so fast, and I was so scared—sweat was pouring down my face, and it felt like I couldn't move. However, I felt that it was my responsibility to (finally) tell them the truth. I mustered up enough nerves and strength to get up and walk to the pulpit.

"As I stood at the podium, I felt as though I was about to pass out. I began to plead for them to sit down and to calm themselves. I stood there for a while until there was a hush all over the church. They needed answers from their pastor, and (for once), I was going to tell them the truth.

"I (first) apologized to them for not being the kind of pastor that should have preached salvation and living holy to them, but instead, I gave them watered-down messages of prosperity and social status. I talked to them from my heart and shared with them what God wanted me to say. I explained to them that those who disappeared had been true believers and that God took them in what was called the rapture of the church because of their faithfulness. I preached a powerful message about how the Bible spoke about this event as a 'secret catching away of the saints from 1 Thessalonians 4:17.' I explained to them not to despair because we still had a chance to repent and get it right.

"When I finished preaching, I made an appeal for those who wanted to repent and give their hearts to the Lord to join me at the altar because I needed to repent as well. Many of them got up out of their seats and ran to the altar. Instead of me praying over them, I stepped down from the pulpit and joined them as we all fell down on our knees and cried out to God to save us. When we got up off of our knees, we hugged each other and cried. Many of them are here in this camp with us.

"There were times, while I was home alone, that I wanted to commit suicide because I was so devastated. My wife and my children were gone. What did I have to live for? But God was faithful and began to strengthen me for the task of ministering to those who were given a second chance.

"From that day until now, I have been totally sold out to the cause of Christ. I am doing what I should have been doing all along. God told me that I was going to minister to people who had gotten left behind, so here I am.

"I met Brother Willie and Sister Betty one day when I was in their store, and we became good friends. They told me about a group of them that were hiding out in the woods because of their faith. They realized that Dr. Benetue Commeme was the Antichrist, and they didn't want to be captured and forced to take the *mark*."

All of a sudden, I recognized where I saw this man before. He was that guest preacher that was on the world news channel in tears, saying the exact same things about how and why he missed the rapture.

I thought to myself, *What an amazing testimony!* As we all sat around the trailer, Pastor Goodman got some wood out of a barrel that was next to him and a long red device, which I realized was a lighter. He put the wood in a pit in front of us and used the red lighter to ignite the fire as Dad and I began to share our testimony with him.

After we talked for a few hours, it was really getting late, and we were all tired. Brother Willie and Sister Betty told us we were welcomed to stay with them in their trailer for however long we needed. I was so glad to hear that because she and Brother Willie were so friendly, and I already started getting close to them. Besides, I still had my mind on that apple pie.

When we got back inside their trailer, the first thing I did was ask Sister Betty if it was too late to get that piece of apple pie. She laughed so hard at me until she bent over at the kitchen table in tears. Brother Willie and my dad joined in laughing as well. I thought to myself, *They can laugh all they want, but I'm getting that piece of pie.* Of course, I laughed along with them.

We all decided to sit at the table and ate apple pie together. It was so good! Sister Betty heated up a pot of coffee for herself and the men, and I was obliged to have a glass of milk.

Afterward, Brother Willie and Sister Betty pulled out some rollaway beds that had been stored in the corner of the living room. They got out some sheets and blankets from the cedar chest in the living room, and Sister Betty motioned for me to help her get our beds ready. Sister Betty gave us some night clothes to change into and we all held hands and prayed, thanking God for his protection and for his mercy. As soon as my head hit the pillow, I dosed right off to sleep.

My and Dad's pullout beds were side by side in the hallway of the trailer. As I sat on the side of the bed, thinking and pondering over our adventurous day, Dad reached across and grabbed my hand and said, "Stacie, are you all right?" I answered, "Yes, Dad, I'm just thinking about our day!" He went on to say, "You know, I am so glad

God placed you in my life. I don't know where I would have been had you not come down the street to my house on that dreadful day to see if I was all right. And I am so glad I am blessed with a daughter who I am very proud of. God placed us in each other's life for such a time as this, honey. I replied, "He sure did, Dad, and I love you so much!"

As soon as my head hit the pillow, I went right off to sleep. I guess I didn't realize how tired I was.

CHAPTER 10

CHURCH IN THE WOODS

The next morning, I woke up startled because I couldn't remember where I was. I sat straight up in the bed, looking around trying to get my bearings. I looked across from me and saw my dad still asleep in his bed. Relieved and realizing that I was safe, I laid my head back down on the pillow and began to thank God for leading us to a safe place.

I looked over at the clock on the stove, and it was 7:00 a.m. I was excited because it was Sunday morning. I thought to myself, *If I was at home, and the rapture hadn't taken place, I would be getting ready for church. Mom would come up the steps to my bedroom singing that annoying song, "Get up, sleepyhead! Get up!"* Oh, how I missed that song that I used to hate and even my mom stomping up the steps (on purpose) to wake me up.

I heard Sister Betty stirring around in the kitchen, and she saw that I was awake, so she whispered and said, "Well, good morning, love! How did you sleep?" I replied, "Like a rock!" She gave me a jovial chuckle and started preparing breakfast. She told me I could get up, get showered, and dressed. She walked over to the cedar chest and handed me a white cotton dress with pink and yellow daisies all over it. It was a little big for me, but it was really cute. She also handed me some undergarments and told me that she often purchased clothing from town just in case someone needed them.

As I showered, the hot water felt so good. Once again, it reminded me of home and my own bathroom shower and how I used to stand under the hot water and let it wash away all of my cares for the moment. When I got out of the shower, I could hear Dad, Brother Willie, and Sister Betty talking. I hurried up and got dressed so that Dad could come in, shower, and get dressed as well. Plus, I was known for being nosey; I wanted to be in on their conversation.

When I came out of the bathroom, Dad had a pair of Brother Willie's pants and a plaid shirt folded up in his arms. As he walked past me, he greeted me with a fatherly "Good morning!" I replied, "Good morning, Dad!" He replied, "I love being called 'Dad.'"

After Dad was showered and dressed, Brother Willie and Sister Betty informed us that after breakfast, we were going to church service. I was shocked because, here, we were living out in the woods. I thought to myself, *Where in the world are we going to go to church?* Sister Betty said, "We usually have services in the big tent around the bend there (pointing out of the kitchen window)." I stood up and looked out of the window and saw a large Army-green-colored tent. I got so excited because I hadn't been to church since the rapture had taken place, so this was going to be wonderful!

Sister Betty placed a platter of bacon, eggs, and toast on the table, and Brother Willie asked Dad if he would bless the table. Dad looked as though he was a little nervous because I was the only person he had ever prayed in front of. He glanced over at me, and I nodded my head to reassure him he could do it. He prayed such a beautiful prayer that it brought tears to my eyes:

"Dear God, we are so grateful for everything you have done for me and Stacie. You gave all of us here in this camp another chance, even though we didn't deserve it. Lord, you rescued me when I was at my lowest and sent me a beautiful daughter so that we both wouldn't be alone. And, Lord, you even blessed us with a whole community of believers as our new family, so we are truly grateful. Now, Lord, bless this food and the hands that prepared it in Jesus's name. *Amen!*"

After Dad's prayer, he sort of looked up with embarrassment on his face, probably wondering if his prayer was suitable. Brother Willie reassured him that it was a wonderful prayer, and we began to eat. While eating, there was a sense of peace in the room. It felt so good sitting at the table laughing and talking with this elderly couple. They reminded me (so much) of my grandparents who had passed away a year apart. I remember when I was ten, my grandfather passed, and then a year later, one day after my eleventh birthday, my grandmother passed away. I was devastated because I really loved them, and I loved to go to Memphis, Tennessee, to visit them in the summer.

After we finished eating breakfast, I helped Sister Betty clear the table and wash the dishes. She told me to just put the dishes in the dish rack on the counter and let them dry. She said we could put them away when we got back from church.

As we walked out of the trailer and down the road toward the large tent where church services were held, we saw some of the couples we had met walking and holding hands; some single people as well as the teens I met. And as we passed them, most of them were walking with their Bibles in their hands. They all greeted us with, "Praise the Lord!"

When we finally got to the tent, we walked through the opening, and I looked around to get my bearings. There were folding chairs arranged in rows. It looked to be about fifty to seventy-five chairs in all with an aisle right down the middle. Brother Willie and Sister Betty motioned for us to follow them so we could sit near the front with them. I looked around trying to see if I recognized anybody. I recognized some of the people we met last night and smiled as we walked past them.

I noticed Pastor Goodman, who we met the day before, sitting in the pulpit area on a cushioned chair reading over his notes. When it was time to start service, he got up from his seat and walked to a makeshift podium. He gave us a warm welcome and told us to pull out the songbook that was in a rack underneath our seats. "Let's open our hymnal to page 378 and sing 'Amazing Grace.' Come on, everybody, stand."

I glanced over at Dad and smiled because he loved to sing those old hymns. I reached under my seat and found the red book. I opened it up to page 378 as directed.

As the organist began to play, we all joined in with the congregation singing:

> Amazing grace, how sweet the sound;
> that saved a wretch like me.
> I once was lost, but now am found;
> was blind but now I see.
> 'Twas grace that taught my heart to fear
> And grace my fears relieved
> How precious did that grace appear
> The hour I first believed.
> When we've been there ten thousand years
> Bright shining as the sun
> We've no less days to sing his praise
> Than when we first began.

The words to that song brought tears to my eyes. They were so powerful. It felt so good to be able to sing as a new Christian and to understand the words of the song. After we finished singing, Pastor Goodman motioned for us to take our seats. He opened his notes and began to speak to us as if he were talking to each one of us one-on-one:

"I am so glad to see each of you this morning. God has spared our lives another day. He has kept us safe and has supplied us with enough food and shelter, for this we are so grateful.

"Let's read Luke 17:26–37. I will be using the NIV translation:

> *Just as it was in the days of Noah, so also will it be in the days of the Son of Man. People were eating, drinking, marrying and being given in marriage up to the day Noah entered the ark. Then the flood came and destroyed them all. It was the same in the days of Lot. People were eating and drink-*

ing, buying and selling, planting and building. But the day Lot left Sodom, fire and sulfur rained down from heaven and destroyed them all. It will be just like this on the day the Son of Man is revealed. On that day no one who is on the housetop, with possessions inside, should go down to get them. Likewise, no one in the field should go back for anything. Remember Lot's wife! Whoever tries to keep their life will lose it, and whoever loses their life will preserve it. I tell you, on that night two people will be in one bed; one will be taken and the other left. Two women will be grinding grain together; one will be taken and the other left. "Where, LORD?" they asked. He replied, "Where there is a dead body, there the vultures will gather."

"This scenario has played out in the mind of each one of you here today. We all have had loved ones who were caught up in the rapture, and it has been very hard and even scary to finally come to terms with ourselves that we were left behind. You know, the terrible thing is that I used to believe in end-time prophecy when I was a young man. When I accepted my calling to the ministry, I was very dedicated to the cause of Christ. Then, as the years went by, I began to backslide. Even though I still would watch different preachers on television preach about the rapture, I pushed it out of my mind. I just didn't believe it would happen so soon. I was so stupid and caught up in worldly things. Being the most popular pastor in Cameron County was my goal. I wanted to have a megachurch with the most members. I actually taught my members that if you placed your name on our church roll, you were saved.

"Boy, was I wrong. Oh, God, was I so wrong. My wife and my kids are gone. My church members who were genuinely saved are gone! And I, the preacher, am left behind. Those of you here today probably have similar testimonies. Some of you were even members of my church. Now, I have to constantly apologize to you because I misled you. Some of you were led to believe that if you gave good tithes and offerings, that was all you needed to do to be saved. Some of you even did volunteer work at your local church or sang in the choir, but that didn't mean you were saved. You had to accept Jesus Christ as your Lord and Savior. Our true born-again family members and friends warned us that this day would happen, but we didn't listen.

"I know that I have preached this message over and over again. Nevertheless, today, I want you to know that, if you are not saved, you have been given a second chance. Today, you can still believe in Jesus Christ and accept him in your heart as Lord and Savior. He is the only way to make it into heaven.

"Now, I must warn you that we are going to have to go through what is called the 'tribulation period.' We are actually living in it right now. It is going to be the roughest time you will ever experience in your life. Listen! We are going to have to keep up with what is going on in the world today and make sure we read our Bibles and stay prayerful. Be faithful to the church services we have set up because they will be your source of strength. We have got to stick together and support one another.

"Last week, I warned you that the new world leader, Dr. Benetue Commeme, is truly the Antichrist. He has set up registration camps all over the world and forcing everyone to accept his mark. Whatever you do, *do not take that mark*! If you do, you will be doomed to hell. Please don't be deceived. One day, we are all going to be discovered out here. We will probably be taken to prison camps, and we will be tortured and martyred because of our faith. But if you stay strong, right at the moment of your death, you will be ushered into heaven by the Holy Angels."

He walked over to the edge of the pulpit area and got down on his knees and said, "Everyone, come to the altar. Those of you who want to give your heart to the Lord, and those who need strength, come pray with me."

I looked around and saw everybody in the congregation get up immediately out of their seats and walked to the altar. As I stood, Dad, Brother Willie, and Sister Betty were all standing as well, and we all began walking toward the altar. Everybody got down on their knees and began crying out to the Lord as Pastor Goodman began praying:

"Repeat this after me! Lord Jesus, we are so sorry that we twisted your Gospel and watered it down. We are so sorry that we ignored your warnings and your loving, beckoning call that we felt in our spirit. I surrender my life to you and invite you into my heart. I will follow you all the days of my life. Please protect us from the danger to come. And if we are captured and face death, let us stand strong and proclaim that we are Christians. And we say hallelujah! We say hallelujah! We worship your holy name."

There was such an anointing in the tent service. God was truly in our midst. I just wanted to stay at that altar and worship. Dad was sitting on the floor enraptured in the spirit with his hands lifted up. Brother Willie and Sister Betty were kneeling and holding hands as they earnestly prayed. Everyone was sobbing, and I believe we all felt that something was about to happen that would change our lives forever. Whatever was about to happen, God was giving us the strength to go through it.

CHAPTER 11

A TRAITOR IN THE CAMP

A few months have passed since the last time I wrote something in this journal. We have been going through our same routine of studying the Bible together, going to church services at the big tent, and just enjoying each other's company. Everyone here in the camp has become one big happy family. I have grown to really love this community, especially Brother Willie and Sister Betty; they were like my grandparents. Sister Betty has been teaching me how to cook and sew. Lately, we have been working on some quilts for our beds. Sister Betty had a trunk full of different scraps of material she had been saving from old dresses, pants, shirts, and old sheets. She showed me how to cut them up into different-sized squares to make the quilts.

She shared with me the story of how the slaves used to make quilts that had special messages hidden in the pattern. She told me that there were two historians that said African American slaves used a quilt code to navigate the Underground Railroad. Some of the quilts had patterns named "wagon wheel," "tumbling blocks," and "bear's paw." These all appeared to have contained secret messages that helped direct the slaves to freedom. She said that their ancestors passed down the secret of the quilt code from one generation to the next.[12] That was so interesting to me because it showed how resilient and brave they were, and I was proud to be a descendent of these heroic people. I got into the habit of sitting down and talking with Sister Betty because she always had wise counsel for me.

We even talked about what heaven was going to be like, and she painted such a beautiful picture of it as we read the description from the Bible. We studied in the book of John 14: 2–3 that heaven had mansions where we would dwell with Jesus.[13] I was so fascinated that the Bible said there would be twelve gates in heaven, which were twelve pearls. Each of the gates was made of a single pearl, and the street of the city was pure gold, transparent as glass.[14] Those moments meant so much to me, and it helped us pass the time away, and I imagined my mom walking down those streets of gold in heaven and praising God.

Dad had become friends with several of the men in the camp. There was a lake behind our trailer, and the men often went fishing together and talked about their lives before the rapture took place. It was always a treat when Dad came back with several fish that he caught because that meant we were going to have a fish fry that night for dinner. Sister Betty would make smothered potatoes with onions in her large skillet to go with the fish and fresh vegetables from a small garden she had in the back of her trailer. *Oh my goodness, it was always so good.*

Recently, we were told that everybody had to take turns going into town (once a month) to try to get food and essentials and bring it back to our camp. It has been getting harder and harder for this task because we can no longer purchase groceries without having the *mark*. Sometimes, some of the store clerks would give Christians a

---

[12] "Did Quilts Hold Codes to the Underground Railroad?" National Geographic, published February 6, 2004, https://www.nationalgeographic.com/culture/article/did-quilts-hold-codes-to-the-underground-railroad#:~:text=Share%20Tweet%20Email-,Two%20historians%20say%20African%20American%20slaves%20may%20have%20used%20a,to%20freedom%2C%20the%20pair%20claim.
[13] John 14: 2–3 (KJV)
[14] Revelation 21:21 (ESV)

break and overlooked those who did not have the *mark*. However, people had been instructed to turn in anyone who didn't have the *mark*, so we had to be very prayerful and resourceful.

Pastor Goodman started visiting every trailer in our camp and praying with each family member for their strength. I enjoyed his visits because it kept us uplifted. After he prayed with us, he indicated that it was our turn to make that dreaded trip to get food for the camp. We have never been selected to go (thus far) because we were new, but now, the lot has fallen on us, so we decided that we would go first thing in the morning. Brother Willie and Sister Betty said they would go with us.

It's funny because, this morning, when we all got dressed and had our breakfast, Sister Betty shared with us that when she woke up, she had an uneasy feeling. She said something was about to happen and that we needed to pray for God's protection. That really frightened me, and I felt sick to my stomach. *What was getting ready to happen to us,* I thought to myself.

I have come to terms with the fact that we were (now) one of the "tribulation saints." I recall on one particular Sunday, Pastor Goodman preached about Christian martyrs. He said that in the book of Revelation, it speaks of a vision that John saw where a vast number of tribulation saints had been martyred by the Antichrist:

> There before me was a great multitude that no one could count, from every nation, tribe, people and language, standing before the throne and in front of the Lamb. They were wearing white robes and were holding palm branches in their hands. (Revelation 7:9)

> When John asks who they are, he said, "These are they who have come out of the great tribulation; they have washed their robes and made them white in the blood of the Lamb." (Revelation 7:14)

That portion of the scripture had been very comforting to me because it encouraged us that if we lose our lives for the cause of Christ, we would still enjoy the splendors of heaven and be with the Lord. I looked forward to seeing my mother and my grandparents.

Every evening, we all gathered together in front of the church tent to watch the world news channel. One of the men here in our community named Brother Tim (who we followed here) had a battery-operated radio and some sort of television set that he could play without it being plugged in. He was very good with technical stuff, and even though we were in a wooded area where the signal was very weak, he had some type of device that allowed him to pick up a signal from very far away.

Today, as we gathered together to watch the news, the commentator came on the air and announced that our leader had an important announcement to make. Dr. Benetue Commeme appeared on the screen, and as I watched, he looked different to me. He still had a handsome olive-colored complexion; however, today, he looked more sinister or demonic. I whispered what I noticed to my dad, and he agreed. The speech that he gave was very frightening. I thought to myself, *Maybe this is why Sister Betty had a foreboding feeling that something was about to happen.* He began to say:

"Good morning to all of you, my beautiful people all over the world. I wish you peace from the universal higher power with whom I have been given authority to govern this entire world. I am so happy to have the opportunity to come on the airways and talk to you. I want to commend you for following my instructions and making sure you register at your local station that we have set up in every neighborhood all over the world. I urge you to keep up the good work of informing my 'special agents' of those you have come in contact with that refuse to take my *mark*. These people are traitors and must be dealt with accordingly. As you know, I have set up special camps for them so that we can deprogram their thinking and release the 'higher power of the universe' into their minds and get rid of their antiquated ways.

"Some of these people who call themselves Christians are still reading and following the teachings of that outdated book they call the Bible. They still believe that those who disappeared on the dreadful day months ago were taken to heaven. They refuse to believe that their loved ones were captured by a UFO, which we have documented proof.

"Therefore, I am declaring and mandating that all Bibles be destroyed in every home. I am burning down every church building that is still standing. Also, I am sending out my special agents to search every home to make sure they do not have any Bibles or religious books that are persuading people to follow its teachings.

"These books will be replaced with our *One World, Good News* book. You see, those Bibles are too critical and invasive of people's personal lifestyles. The higher power of the universe is not a judging force, but it is gentle and accepting of all people and all beliefs. I suggest that if you have one of these Bibles or religious material, please get rid of it so that we will all be together serving a true one-world religion."

We were in total shock. He was actually going to destroy all Bibles from every home in the entire world.

I am so glad that there were still copies of the Bible that had been left after the rapture. Pastor Goodman, Brother Willie, and Sister Betty shared with us how they made sure they smuggled as many Bibles as they could into our camp because they knew we were going to need them. They distributed these Bibles and religious books to every family in our little community.

Pastor Goodman told us that there were actually many underground Bible study groups all over the world who had smuggled Bibles in containers, pages rolled up and hidden in bottles, and some have even hidden pages in their shoes. When people realized that they had been left behind after the rapture, they sought out Bibles to read and to see if what happened to their loved ones was really prophesied in the Bible and what they needed to do to be saved.

Pastor Goodman encouraged all of us to be brave and to serve the Lord Jesus Christ with our whole heart, even in the midst of facing the tribulation. I knew that I had to be faithful to the end and that many of us were going to die for our faith. However, in our death, I knew that we would be victorious. The Bible said:

They overcame (Satan) by the blood of the Lamb and by the word of their testimony; they did not love their lives so much as to shrink from death. (Revelation 12:11)

And God will reward them: "He who sits on the throne will spread his tent over them. Never again will they hunger; never again will they thirst. The sun will not beat upon them, nor any scorching heat. For the Lamb at the center of the throne will be their shepherd; he will lead them to springs of living water. And God will wipe away every tear from their eyes." (Revelation 7:15–17)

Tomorrow's going to be our family's turn to go out and forage for food for the camp. I have a nervous feeling in the pit of my stomach today. Dad informed me that he didn't have a clue how we were going to pull it off since they had been rounding up Christians and putting them in deprograming camps. Brother Tim said he wanted to go with us because he knew some places we could go to where they would help us.

Lately, for some reason, I began not to trust Brother Tim. Even though we need his radio and television to keep up with the latest world news, he just strikes me as not being trustworthy. One day, when he was setting up his equipment, he started getting a little hot because he had on a heavy jacket. He took off his jacket and laid it on the seat next to him. He had on a short-sleeved shirt, and I noticed that there was something on his arm, sort of like some type of blue and red symbol or a tattoo. When he caught me glancing at it, he hurried up and put his jacket back on. I began to think, *What is he hiding? What was so secretive about that tattoo?* Now, ever since that day, I catch him staring at me as if he is trying to read my thoughts about him. I kept this incident to myself, but (lately), I feel compelled to tell somebody.

After dinner, we all decided we needed to go to bed early so that we would have a clear head tomorrow. Dad gathered me, Brother

Willie, and Sister Betty together at the kitchen table to discuss our strategy. He said he was glad that he still had a considerable amount of gas in his car so that we wouldn't have to worry about running out. Tomorrow, we're going to drive into town and stake out places where we think people would be kind not to turn us in. We were going to have to trust God to lead us where we could go. Brother Tim said he wanted to go with us because he had some friends and acquaintances that might help us.

We all joined hands, and Brother Willie led us in prayer. After the prayer, we all put on our nightclothes and went to bed. As I lay in my cot next to my dad's, I saw a tear running down his cheek. "Dad, are you okay?" I said in a whisper. He answered and said, "Honey, I promised God that I would take care of you, and I don't want to lead us in any danger tomorrow. But I know God has a plan for us, and we have to trust him no matter what we have to face." He reached over and grabbed my hand and squeezed it tight. He held my hand until we both drifted off to sleep.

CHAPTER 12

WE CAN'T GO BACK HOME

Today, we all woke up and ate a hearty breakfast that Sister Betty put together. Things have been getting a little scarce lately, and we had been rationing our food and eating smaller portions; however, today, she decided to splurge and cooked us a nice breakfast. She said that we needed strength for our journey. We cleared the table, washed the dishes, and put them away. Everyone seemed extra quiet and engaged in their thoughts. Brother Willie finally broke the silence and said, "Well, I guess it's time to go. Are we ready?" We all said yes together.

We walked out of the trailer and down the steps toward the parking lot where our car was. Dad and Brother Willie got in the front, and Sister Betty and I got in the back. We drove a few yards to where Brother Tim's trailer was. When we pulled up in front, Dad tooted his horn, and Brother Tim came out of his trailer almost trotting down his four steps.

He opened the door on my side of the car and got in. For some reason, I did not want that man sitting next to me; however, I slid over in the middle next to Sister Betty. Brother Tim had a nervous laugh as he sat down next to me and greeted us, "Good morning, my people! Let's do this! Let's do this!" He had a bunch of maps and papers in his arms as he got in the car. He reminded me of a "nerdy professor" fumbling and dropping papers on the floor. In my mind, I was thinking, *I don't trust this man! I should have said something. I should've told Dad, Brother Willie, and Sister Betty about my fears last night when we were sitting around the table and talking about our strategy.*

As Dad backed up the car and pulled out of the camp, I looked straight in front of me as we headed to town. I didn't want to look at Brother Tim. I felt a sinister presence in the car coming from him. I began praying under my breath for protection. I could see his facial expressions out of the corner of my left eye, and he looked as though he was smiling. His smile reminded me of Dr. Benetue Commeme when he came on air to address the world. He had that same sinister smirk on his face.

The ride to town seemed longer than I thought, probably because of Brother Tim in the car. Sister Betty either slept all the way or was praying because she kept her eyes closed. When we finally got into town, Brother Tim opened up one of his maps and started looking at it. I glanced at it, and I noticed he had red marks and blue marks on different areas. He told my dad that he marked stores that might be safe to get food. He said that he knew people who took the *mark* but were still friendly and willing to help us. He said, "Let's try Silver's Market and Poultry. I know them quite well there. They were friends of my parents." He directed us to where the store was located, and we pulled up in the parking lot. It looked fairly safe, but I did notice that there were customers in the store. Dad suggested that we wait in the car until the customers left.

We sat in the car for about twenty minutes. Then, Brother Tim said, "I think it's safe to go in now." Sister Betty began praying, "Lord, we are your servants. Please protect us and give us strength for this task in Jesus's name. Amen!" We all chimed in saying amen, or should I say, we all said amen except Brother Tim. He told us to follow his lead as we got out of the car and walked behind him into the store.

The man at the counter looked friendly and gave us a warm greeting, "Hello, how are you all this fine day?" Brother Tim told him we were here to get groceries and essentials. He then asked the man a question, "Are you one of the helpers of the brethren?" I thought to myself, *Who in the world is "the helpers of the brethren"? What is this secret between these two men?* The man gave Brother Tim a wink and said, "Ah, yes, yes! You all help yourselves to whatever you need, it's on me!"

Brother Willie gave the man a sturdy handshake and got a grocery cart from the front of the store, and he and Sister Betty began shopping. Dad got another cart and said he was going to get essentials like toothpaste, toilet paper, soap, and deodorant. He told me to help him get the items. Brother Tim stayed in the front talking to the man at the counter. When I got Dad alone, I began to share with him how I felt about Brother Tim. I told him about the incident with the tattoo and how he stared at me in a sinister kind of way. I was glad Dad didn't dismiss my concerns and told me he was going to keep an eye on him. We went down the aisles where we found most of the things we needed that would accommodate everyone in our camp. Brother Willie and Sister Betty had a cart full of meat, canned goods, milk, juice, bread, and sugar. I was worried that we had too much and would be told to put some of the items back by the owner of the store since he was donating them to us.

When we got to the counter, the man was very kind and told us we were okay, and he helped us bag up our groceries. The men shook hands and thanked him for helping us. Dad offered to pray for him, and he had the strangest look on his face. He looked at Brother Tim and said, "For the universe, man! For the universe!" Brother Tim responded by giving him a high five. Dad just prayed a quick prayer thanking God for the man being so generous. I thought to myself, *For the universe? What in the world did they mean?* I just dismissed it.

We walked out of the store (cautiously) carrying the groceries. I glanced across the street and noticed that there was a building on the corner with a sign that read Registration Station set up on the corner. I tapped my dad and pointed in that direction and said, "Look, Dad, that's one of those places that gives you the *mark*." He whispered to me, "Honey, stop pointing! I don't want to call attention to us. Let's just act normal, put these groceries in the trunk, and get out of here."

I and Sister Betty got in the car first. The men put the groceries in the trunk and got in. I turned around and looked back at the man in the store from our rear window. As we started to drive away, I noticed that he was talking on the phone. My flesh felt cold and sweaty. I thought, *I wonder who he's talking to? Was he calling the special guards on us?* Dad noticed it too and mentioned it to Brother Tim; however, Brother Tim reassured us that we were safe and that the man was his friend, and we didn't need to be concerned. I didn't trust him, and I gave my dad that look. He knew exactly what I was thinking, and I believe he was thinking the same thing.

The drive back to our camp was long and quiet; we kept seeing black official cars speeding past us with the special guard emblem on them. Some of the cars even slowed down, and the men would peer into our car with stern looks on their faces. I whispered a prayer for God to let us get back to the camp safe and sound.

When we finally got back to the camp, Dad drove up to the big church tent where we were going to meet up with all of the campers and divvy out the groceries. I was so glad nothing eventful happened to us. My nerves were really on edge after that adventure, but I was glad we were able to get food and essentials for everybody in the camp. Brother Willie told Pastor Goodman, "We were able to get a lot of groceries from that store, and the man didn't even charge us anything because he said that we had to have the *mark* so he could scan our hand or forehead to take the money out of our bank account. Dad said, "The cashless society has begun! In order for the Antichrist or the beast to control all buying and selling (Revelation 13:17), a cashless society will be necessary during the tribulation. As long as people are using cash, transactions can be completed in private, but if all currency becomes electronic, then every transaction can be monitored.[15]"

Dad and Brother Willie gave instructions for every family representative to meet us at the church tent. When everybody gathered, they were to form two lines. Pastor Goodman had a couple of cases of

---

[15] "Does a cashless society have anything to do with the end times?" Got Questions, ww.gotquestions.org/cashless-society.html.

medium-sized boxes that needed to be put together and taped with some strong strapping tape. I and Brother Tim volunteered to do that task while Dad, Brother Willie, and Sister Betty said they would fill up the boxes after we put them together and hand them to those that were in line. I really didn't want to work with Brother Tim, but I felt that I needed to keep an eye on him.

As we were putting the boxes together, the motion of bending down, standing back up, setting the boxes on the table, forcing the corners together, and taping them was a little tedious. I found myself sweating and getting a little dehydrated. Brother Tim seemed to be sweating as well, and (once again), he took off his jacket and rolled up his shirt sleeves. This time, I got a good look at that tattoo on his left arm and made a mental picture of it in my mind so that I could sketch it in my journal. Lately, I have been keeping my journal with me hidden inside my jacket pocket. I made an excuse to Brother Tim that I needed to go to the restroom. Once inside, I got out my journal and ink pen. It was one of those pens that had three different colors you could choose from. I hurriedly sketched out what that tattoo looked like in full color so that I wouldn't forget.

As I began to sketch out the tattoo in my journal, it suddenly dawned on me that Brother Tim's tattoo had the same symbol that was on all of the cars of the special guards and the symbol of the One World United. I thought to myself, *Oh my god! That's where I saw that symbol. Brother Tim had the mark of the beast on his arm. He is one of the Antichrist's secret servicemen.*

I didn't know what to do. I stood there in the bathroom actually hyperventilating and looking at myself in the mirror. I kept saying, *Stacie, girl, you got to pull yourself together. You can't let Brother Tim know you are on to him.* I broke out in a cold sweat, and my legs felt like rubber bands. Somehow, I had to get to Dad and tell him what I discovered. I put my journal back in the inside pocket of my jacket and turned the water faucet on at the sink. I cupped my hands together and drank some water and then put water on my face so that I could calm myself down.

I walked back out in the tent and joined Brother Tim where we were stationed and continued to work on assembling boxes. He looked at me and said, "I was wondering what happened to you. I thought I was going to have to send in the cavalry after you." He leaned back and laughed, and I could see a demonic presence on his face. I began to pray under my breath for protection. I realized that I needed to (somehow) tell my dad what I had just witnessed.

I grabbed a couple of the finished boxes and took them over to my dad and the other crew at that assembly line so that they could fill the boxes with food and some of the essentials. I gave my dad a signal with my eyes to look over at Brother Tim's arm. At first, Dad couldn't figure out what in the world I was trying to tell him. He kept frowning at me like he was asking me, "What?" I knew I couldn't whisper it or say anything with my lips because I didn't want Brother Tim to notice.

Dad finally understood what I was trying to get him to do, and he glanced over at Brother Tim's arm. He stood there with a puzzled look on his face, and I prayed, *God, please reveal to him what I am trying to get him to see.* After a while, it looked like he got it. He nodded at me as if he understood. He closed his eyes, and I could tell he was praying.

The first man who had been in line to get a box of food had walked out of the tent to take his box back to his trailer; however, all of a sudden, he came running back in, all out of breath, and said, "Black cars have surrounded the tent! They sneaked up on us with their lights turned off. It looks like it's about five or six cars. We have been discovered!"

Everybody in the tent began to panic. Pastor Goodman got our attention and motioned for us to calm down and began to speak to us, "Okay! Okay! Calm down, everybody! Calm down! This is the day I warned all of you would happen. Let's all gather here at the altar and pray for strength to face whatever is before us. God wants us to be strong and to not cave under pressure." We all walked toward the altar, and I grabbed my dad's hand as we all knelt down together. Pastor Goodman began to pray:

"Lord, you said you are our refuge and our strength. You said you are a very present help in trouble.[16] We are in trouble right now and we need your strength to face what is going to happen next. Give us the stamina to say no to our captors. Give us the strength to refuse to take the MARK. If we have to die, give us the courage to face it with dignity. Holy Spirit, stand up in us! Be our guide!"

As we all were gathered at the altar, I could hear footsteps coming into the tent. I glanced out of the corner of my eye and saw men dressed in all black coming in with rifles in their hands pointing at us. It looked like there were about ten to fifteen men. They began to surround us so that no one would try to run. I heard a familiar voice telling us to stand up and put our hands on the back of our head. It was Brother Tim. He spoke to the men and said, "What took you guys so long? I thought you weren't coming." One of the men laughed and said, "Man, we got lost! This place was hard to find, especially at night. We kept missing our turn." Brother Tim began to laugh with that sinister grin on his face.

Pastor Goodman spoke and said, "Son, why would you betray us? We have been very good to you. I took you in and helped you when you said you needed shelter." Brother Tim answered him with the most sinister answer, "If you fool with a snake, you will get bitten!" He and the other men began to laugh as he told us to get up from the floor. They made us line up with our hands behind our heads. Dad stayed close to me so that I wouldn't be afraid, and Brother Willie and Sister Betty walked together.

For some reason, I wasn't afraid. It was as if that prayer fortified us for what we were about to face. I realized that God had warned us ahead of time about Brother Tim and his betrayal.

---

[16] Psalm 46:1(KJV)

As they marched us out of the tent, I felt an unction from God to take my journal out of my inside jacket pocket. So while no one was looking, I took it out, and slipped it down in my underpants; the legs of my underpants were kind of snug so I didn't have to worry about the journal falling out. It made me walk a little funny, but I don't think the men in black noticed.

They opened the car doors and loaded us in different cars. I am so glad that they put me and my dad in the car together. The cars all had three rows of seats in them, so they packed us in all of the cars. The man that was driving our car pulled out what looked like a sophisticated walkie-talkie. He pushed the red button on the side of the device and said, "Mission accomplished." Brother Tim got in the front on the other side of the driver. I wondered why he got in our car, probably because Pastor Goodman was in the car, and he wanted to humiliate him.

All of the black cars that they had us in pulled out of the camp one by one, and we started driving down those dark roads until we got to the highway. Dad reached over and grabbed my hand and whispered, "Be strong, honey! Be strong!" I nodded and squirmed in my seat to readjust the book I had tucked away in my underpants. It was very uncomfortable, but I made it work. I didn't want them to discover it because I wanted to document everything we were getting ready to go through. I always said, "If I had to die, I wanted to make sure that someone who was a tribulation Christian would find this journal and read it for strength." I believe that was why God had me write in my journal.

CHAPTER 13

THE DEPROGRAMMING CAMP

The drive seemed long, and I really had no idea where we were going. Brother Tim handed us some burgundy scarfs and told us to put them on to cover our eyes. I figured they didn't want us to see where we were going. Dad tied my scarf on my eyes first; he put on his and grabbed my hand again. I began to wonder how Brother Willie and Sister Betty were handling everything. They were elderly, and I didn't want anything to happen to them, (at least) not yet!

When we finally arrived at our destination, I could hear gravel and rocks as our car tires were rolling over them. When we finally came to a stop, I heard our car door open up, and we were ordered to get out with our hands behind our heads. I could hear doors opening and closing from the other cars as well. They lined us all up, and the men began snatching our blindfolds off of our faces. When they took mine off, I had to blink to refocus my eyes as I held my dad's hand tight.

The place they took us looked like some sort of army barracks. There was a very tall barbed-wire fence surrounding the place. They marched us inside what looked like the headquarters building. We walked past a big and tall dark-skinned man with his belly hanging over his pants. He had on a black uniform with a lot of badges on it, so I figured he must have been a high-ranking soldier or something.

The man ordered the men in black to line us all up against the walls, and he told them to search us. I was so scared that they were going to find my journal. The men began to parade up and down all of us, searching everybody in the line. As they got closer and closer to me, I began to pray under my breath, "Lord Jesus, please don't let them find my journal! Please, God, protect us!" When they got to my dad, they patted him down, handling him very roughly. They made him turn around and face the wall as they searched him thoroughly.

I was the next one to be searched. As the man began to search me, he said, "Take off that jacket," in a mean, deep voice. I took off my jacket (trembling) and handed it to him. He patted it down and searched the outside pockets and then began to look on the inside. He discovered that I had a hidden pocket inside. He stuck his hand down in the pocket and pulled out an old piece of chewing gum covered in lint. I really didn't even know it was there at the bottom of my pocket. He showed it to one of the men in black, and they laughed hysterically. He was so tickled about the gum that he forgot to pat me down to see if I had anything else on me and just moved on to the next person in line. I whispered under my breath, "Thank you, Jesus! You are so faithful!"

After they searched every one of us from the camp, they told us to line up again "single file" and to follow this woman who also had on a black uniform. She seemed a little more kind and motioned for us to follow her down this long hallway. The lights in the hallway were very dim, and the floors were shining like glass. When we got to the end of the hall, we continued to follow her as she turned down another hall where there were a lot of (what looked like) jail cells lined on each side of the hallway.

As we passed by the cells, there were people inside of them peeking out through the bars. Several of the people whispered as we passed, "The peace of God be with you," and some were saying, "Be strong, my brothers and sisters! Be strong!" One of the men in black who was following along behind us with his gun began to yell at the people in their cells to be quiet and began to use the barrel of his gun to pound on their fingers while they were holding the cell bars.

When we finally got to one section of the cells, one of the men in black grabbed my dad and Pastor Goodman, opened the cell door, pushed them in with two of the other men from our camp, and locked the door. I began to cry and plead with the woman who was in charge of the women from our camp to please let me be with my dad. She looked a little sympathetic and told me that those were the men's barracks and that I had to stay with the women.

The man (in anger) pushed me and said, "Shut up and keep walking." We walked down about two hallways and finally reached the barracks where the women were housed. They put me in a cell with two other women from our camp, and to my surprise, they pushed Sister Betty in the cell after me. I whispered, "Thank you, Jesus!"

The cell had four bunk beds with thin grey blankets on them and white pillows and sheets. The beds looked (somewhat) clean and made up neatly. There were a couple of wooden tables with chairs in two of the corners of the room, a toilet in one of the other corners with a makeshift curtain in front of it for privacy, and a sink. Sister Betty was told to take one of the bottom bunks, and I was instructed to take the top bunk that was above her bed.

The lady in black told us she was going to go get us some uniforms and that she would be back. She told us her name was Debbie and that she would be our guard. When she left, Sister Betty grabbed me and hugged me. She told me how much she loved me and that she wanted me to be strong. She began to pray, and the other two ladies in our cell, who were from our camp, asked if they could join in. We all grabbed each other's hands, formed a circle, and prayed for God to strengthen us.

After the prayer, we all sat on our beds and waited for Debbie to come back. I discretely reached in my underpants when no one was looking and got out my journal and hurriedly tucked it away under my pillow.

When the guard named Debbie finally came back, she was carrying some bright orange uniforms that were neatly folded in her arms and some white undergarments. It reminded me of a movie where people were in prison and had on orange uniforms.

Our uniforms consisted of a long-sleeved shirt with a pocket on the top right side, and the pockets had a number on it; matching long pants with a drawstring at the waist so that they could be adjusted to our size; underpants; and a sleeveless undershirt. They all smelled like detergent, so (at least) they were clean.

Debbie (the guard) told us she was going to take us to where we had to shower, so we followed her down the hallway as we carried our uniforms. She took us to a room that had several showerheads in the middle of the ceiling. There were no doors or curtains covering the showers for privacy, just showerheads sunken into the ceiling and drains on the floor so that the water could run down.

There were lockers and benches on one side of the room, and the lady told us to choose a locker and put our uniforms in there until we finished showering. She pointed to us and told us to take off our street clothes. We each took off our clothes and handed them to Debbie. I felt a little ashamed because we were all naked, and I think Sister Bettie was embarrassed as well. Debbie took our street clothes and walked over to a large plastic bin and threw all of our clothes in it. She handed each of us a towel and a bar of soap and told us to get under one of the showerheads.

Debbie pushed a large silver button on the wall, and all of a sudden, the water began to flow from all of the showerheads in the ceiling. The water felt soothing and hot. It reminded me of my shower at home and the one at Brother Willie and Sister Betty's trailer. As I stood there under the shower, I began to wonder how my dad and Brother Willie were doing. *Would I ever get to see them again? Are they okay?* I had a feeling that God was going to let us see each other again.

After we took our showers, Debbie handed us some towels that were not very soft but smelled clean. We all dried off and went to our lockers and put on our uniforms. She (then) handed us a pair of white socks and a pair of orange "flip-flops" to wear on our feet. I kind of laughed to myself, *Well, at least we are color coordinated.*

Debbie led us back to our cell and opened it up. She had a large key ring with several keys on them. She motioned for us to go in, and once we all got inside, she left, locking the bars behind her. Sister Betty waited until I used the edge of her bed to climb up to the top bunk. The other ladies got in their beds, and the lights were turned off by one of the female guards who was sitting at some sort of workstation down the hallway.

As I lay there in my bed just pondering on our eventful day, I wanted to write in my journal, but it was dark. However, I did notice that there was a little bit of light coming from a ceiling light in the hallway. I waited until my eyes adjusted to the dark and took advantage of that small light in the hallway and began to write about our long and exhausting day.

CHAPTER 14

THE BIG DECISION

Today, we were awakened by a loud ringing noise or some sort of siren. We all sat straight up in our beds (startled), not knowing what was happening or what to expect. I hurriedly tucked my journal inside my pillowcase, and we all waited for someone to come to our cell with instructions. Pretty soon, Debbie (the guard) came and unlocked our cell. Sister Betty asked her what we were about to do, and she politely answered and told us we were going to have breakfast, and then later in the evening, she was going to come back and escort us to the deprogramming room. Sister Margaret began to question her about what the deprogramming room was, and Debbie said she couldn't tell us anything except that we were going to be questioned about our faith.

We followed her down the long hallway to the cafeteria. As we walked in, I saw a lot of people sitting on benches at several long tables. There was a lady in the lunchroom that handed us a tray and told us to get in line. I looked around the room to see if I knew anybody from our camp. My eyes spotted my dad and Pastor Goodman sitting across from each other at one of the tables. Then, I spotted Brother Willie sitting at a table across from them. They had their heads bowed down as they were eating. I felt so relieved that they were okay. I tapped Sister Betty and began to whisper to her that

I saw our family. The lady who handed us our trays shouted, "No talking! Keep moving!'

Sister Betty smiled as if to let me know she spotted the men too as we began to move up in the serving line. The ladies that were dishing out the food had on beige uniform dresses with white socks and white gym shoes on. They had on aprons and some type of heavy hairnet on their head, probably for sanitary purposes.

As we moved up in the serving line, the servers started putting food on our trays, a carton of milk, some very dry-looking scrambled eggs, toast, and a bowl of slimy oatmeal. It didn't look very enticing; however, I thought I'd better eat whatever they gave me to keep up my strength.

When we finally got our food, we waited to see what our next instructions were going to be because we didn't want to do the wrong thing and be punished. One of the guards who stood in the corner of the room motioned for us to go to the table we were assigned to. I noticed that the men and teen boys were seated on one side of the cafeteria, and the women and teen girls were made to sit on the opposite side. I noticed that my dad had spotted us as well and gave me a smile and a "thumbs up" sign. *Oh, how I wanted to run over to him and just put my arms around my dad and Brother Willie and Pastor Goodman.*

As we began to eat, I hit my knee on something under our table. It hurt really bad, so I bent down to look under the table to see what I hit my knee on. I noticed that there was some kind of a shelf underneath the table. I eased my hand into the shelf and found a piece of paper that someone had tucked away there. I hurried up and grabbed it and put it in my shirt sleeve. I didn't want one of the guards to see me reading it, so I figured the buttons on my sleeve would prevent it from falling back out and that I would wait and examine it later when we got back to our cell.

While we were eating, we were instructed not to talk to each other and to keep our heads down while we ate. The room felt so quiet and a little eerie. I made sure I ate everything on my tray because I was pretty hungry and because I wanted to stay physically strong.

When we finished eating, we had to sit there, look straight ahead, and wait for further instructions from the guards. Finally, one of the guards came into the cafeteria, spoke in a microphone, and instructed all of us to get up and line up single file and follow our guards back to our cell. One of the male guards was in charge of the men and motioned for them to get up from their tables. Debbie came in and motioned for the women in her wing to follow her back down the long hallway to our cells.

Once we got back to our cell, I waited until Debbie had left, and the coast was clear. We sat down at the table in one of the corners of our cell. I whispered, "Hey you guys, take a look at this." I pulled out the little piece of paper from my sleeve, and we began to examine it. It was a piece of paper that had been laminated. The corners were squared, and it looked a little worn as if it had been in a lot of people's hands.

As we began reading it, we realized that it was a little Bible tract. I wondered who put the tract under the table and how many hands had it gone through before. It had a writing on one side and a picture of people praying and looking up to the sky on the other side.

We all began to read the tract together, and the words were very simple and inspiring. It read:

> If you have been unfortunate enough to have been left behind after the rapture of the church, please:
>
> *Refuse the mark* and *refuse to worship the Antichrist* or his image at any cost (Revelation 13:15–17). It is far better to suffer for a little while now and soon be with Christ than to escape suffering by yielding to the beast and suffer the torments of hell forever (Revelation 14:11).
>
> Be of good courage. Hold fast the Word of God. "He that shall *endure* unto the end, the same shall be saved." (Matthew 24:13)
>
> Perhaps, even now, as you are reading this tract, the rapture has already taken place, and

you are left. Look to him, Jesus Christ, for the strength and courage to suffer for him for he suffered for you even unto death.

The Bible bears testimony that, during this period, you can neither buy nor sell without the mark of the beast, and this will bring great suffering and death to those who refuse the mark. *But he that receives the mark is eternally damned. Be strong! Heaven awaits you!*

I realized that I didn't even know the other two ladies in our cell's names. We would often see each other at the camp and at our tent church services, but now that we were sharing the same cell, we needed to know each other's name, so we formally introduced ourselves.

One of the ladies said her name was Margaret. She had a very kind face and was a short stocky lady with a gap in her front teeth. She looked to be in her fifties and had salt-and-pepper-colored hair. She told me that she was a widow and that her grown children turned on her because she was a Christian. The other lady was young and seemed to be a few years older than me, maybe in her early twenties. She said her name was Lisa, but people called her "Pebbles." I thought that was so cute.

After reading the tract, we all came to the conclusion that the message had to be from God to give us a source of comfort and a reminder to be strong for what we were going to have to face. We all made a promise that we were going to read and study it daily.

After we read the tract several times and discussed it like we were in Bible study, we (somehow) needed to figure out how to share it with the men from our camp. I tucked it away in my journal for safekeeping, looking through the bars of our cell and down the hallway to make sure no one was watching us. We all bowed our heads and began to pray and thank God for showing us that he was still with us. After our prayer, we lay down in our beds for a nap.

We were awakened by Debbie coming down the hall with her large ring of keys jingling in her hand. We all sat up on our beds as she opened our cell door and told us to line up in the hall against the wall. When we obeyed her orders and lined up against the wall, I noticed that there were quite a few women already in the hall in line in front of us.

Debbie led us down the long hallway past the cafeteria into a large room with at least a hundred metal-green folding chairs and several tables across the front of the room with four chairs at each table. There were some kind of machines on every table, and there were notebooks and ink pens in a jar on the tables.

There were two men talking in front of the room with their backs toward us as we entered, so I couldn't see their faces. Debbie told us to find a seat, so we found some empty chairs in the middle of the room and sat down. I noticed that there was a curtain dividing the large room, and I could hear men's voices on the other side of the curtain. I figured that the men from our camp were on that side of the room with other men. I thought to myself, *Oh, God, we are about to have our faith tested, I can feel it!* I said a quick prayer under my breath, "Lord, give us the strength to go through whatever we are about to face."

One of the men who had their backs turned away from us walked over to the wall near the curtain and pushed a button. The curtains began to retract, and we could see the men on the other side of the room.

When the other man that had been talking in front of the room finally turned around and faced us, I almost choked on my own saliva when I saw who he was. I was flabbergasted because it was Brother Tim! I could not believe it! He truly was a traitor. All of the suspicions and fears that I had about him were true. I couldn't believe how he fooled everyone in our camp that long.

He walked up to the microphone and began to speak, "I give honor to our beloved leader, His Grace, Dr. Benetue Commeme. Let us stand in allegiance to this great man." All of a sudden, a screen came down from the ceiling, and a huge picture of Commeme appeared on the screen. All of the guards and special men and women in black stood up and began to clap, cheer, and whistle. It looked like there were about seventy-five to a hundred of them in total. They were all in total ecstasy as if they were worshipping Dr. Commeme. Those of us who were Christians did not stand because we refused to give obeisance to this "man of perdition."

Brother Tim began to introduce himself and said, "I am Timothy Warlock, and I am the chief commander of this local brigade. I have been chosen to carry out the mandates of our great leader to make sure we are all 'one' in unity and beliefs.

"You all are here this evening because you do not share our belief system, and you have refused to adhere to the laws of our 'One World United' government. We cannot and will not tolerate disloyalty. We want to make sure everybody all over the world has embraced our doctrine. The old ways are no longer being taught; all of those antiquated thoughts and ideas about some faraway God who judges people and makes them feel ashamed and guilty are no longer relevant. We are moving forward with the revelation that was given to our leader by the higher power of the universe."

The guards and the men and women in black began applauding and screaming, "All power to Benetue Commeme! All power to Benetue Commeme. He is our savior!" Timothy began to clap and join them shouting in the microphone saying, "Yes, he is our savior, he has been given all power to carry out the universal mandate by the higher power of the universe."

He went on to say, "The first thing I want to do is coerce those of you who didn't stand to stand in honor of our great leader. If you don't stand, our special agents will assist you in standing."

Timothy gave them orders to "carry out their assigned tasks." The next thing I knew, all of the men and women in black got up and started pulling out their batons and began moving in between the rows, standing in front of us and demanding that we all stand in reverence of Commeme or be beaten with their batons. They started grabbing our arms and snatched me, Sister Betty, Margaret, and Pebbles out of our chairs. Sister Betty refused to stand, and one of the men hit her in the head with his baton and knocked her down to the floor. I began to scream and cry, "Sister Betty! Sister Betty!" She lay there on the floor with her head bleeding until Pebbles reached down, picked her up, and set her back down in her chair as Sister Betty began rocking and holding her head in total agony.

Still, she refused to stand and worship Commeme's image. We all followed suit and sat back down in our seats as well, which seemed to make Timothy furious.

One of the ladies in black stepped over a chair that had fallen in front of me and grabbed me by my hair. She pulled my head down to her face and said in a sinister voice, "If you don't stand, I swear, I will kill you!" She said it with such venom and hate in her voice and snatched me up out of my chair. She held me up with her right arm and forced me to stand. I noticed that the other guards did the same thing to all of us who refused to stand.

I glanced over on the other side of the room to see what was happening to my dad, Pastor Goodman, and Brother Willie. I didn't see them at first, but then I noticed that they were lined up against the wall and were being beaten with batons. Dad had his hands over his face to shield the blows, and I saw Pastor Goodman and Brother Willie being knocked down to the floor. They were being hit with the baton over and over again and kicked. It was a terrible sight to see. I began to pray out loud, "Jesus, please help us! Please help us! Give us strength, Lord! Give us strength!"

All of a sudden, one of the men who were from our camp stood up and began singing, "Amazing grace, how sweet the sound that saved a wretch like me." He reached down and lifted up Pastor Goodman, my dad, and Brother Willie from the floor. Then all of the other men in the room began to help each other stand up on their feet and joined in singing.

One by one, Christians all over the room began to reach down and help each other from the floor and stood up. We all locked arms together in solitude and joined in together singing, "I once was lost, but now am found, was blind, but now I see." Some of them had blood running down their faces, but it was as if the Holy Spirit was giving each of us strength. We all joined in singing together in perfect harmony. It seemed as though we were in the presence of angels joining in and singing with us.

Timothy started screaming, "Stop that singing! Stop that singing! We will not tolerate your resistance!" but we sang even louder. I reached over and grabbed Sister Betty's arm, and she (in turn) locked arms with Margaret, and Margaret with Pebbles. Every one of us in that room who were followers of Jesus Christ began to show them the power of God in action. They were not going to discourage us for our faith. I felt the Holy Spirit come over me, and I began to sing in the spirit and was oblivious to my pain.

Timothy began to shout, "Guards, take these people to the deprogramming stations. We are going to show them we mean business! Do it now! We cannot have this insurrection, not on my watch. I am ordering every special guard in this room to grab one of these idiots and take them to the tables so that we can deprogram them!"

The next thing I knew, the lady that had grabbed my arm and threatened me grabbed me again and began pushing me toward the front of the room at one of the tables. I was separated from Sister Betty, Margaret, and Pebbles. The funny thing was, I had no more fear. I felt a holy boldness inside because God had stepped in and gave all of us strength when we were singing so that we could face whatever we were about to face.

As the guard continued to push me down the rows of chairs and the aisle, she shoved me into a chair at one of the tables in the front with the strange machines on them. I spotted my dad as one of the guards was "literally" dragging him to one of the tables. He looked over at me and yelled, "Be strong, honey! Be strong! God is with us!" The man that was dragging my dad kicked him and told him to *shut up and sit down.* He pushed my dad into the chair and shoved his chair under the table.

I realized that it had to be one of the machines they used to give people the *mark of the beast.* It had that same symbol that Timothy had on his arm and that was on the cars that the special agents drove.

I looked around to see if I spotted my cellmates, but I didn't see them. One of the men in black who sat on the other side of the table in front of me began talking to me and asking me a whole lot of questions. He asked me my name and what my beliefs were. I told him, "My name is Stacie Mitchell, and I am a Christian."

He began to laugh, and he said, "What is a Christian? How can you believe in an old-antiquated belief system that excludes other people and doesn't teach the truth? Your God is prejudiced. According to your Bible, he hates people of different religious beliefs and thoughts. Our god is the only universal power, and he accepts everybody no matter what faith."

I told him, "Our God is the only true and living God. And because he created us, he knows what is best for us. He hates sin because it pollutes our bodies and corrupts our minds. He loved us so much that he sent his only son Jesus Christ to become our Savior to save us from our sins."

He chided back at me, "So you are saying that you refuse to accept the teachings of your leader, Dr. Benetue Commeme? You are willing to die for this ridiculous religious belief? You are a young lady. You have your whole life ahead of you. Don't you want to go to college, get a good job, date, or maybe even get married and have children of your own?"

I got even bolder about my God. I answered him and said, "Yes, I am willing to die for my faith. The man you are talking about, Benetue Commeme, is the Antichrist, and I refuse to give my allegiance to him. I would rather die and go to heaven and be with the other saints who got raptured than to accept his *mark* and be damned to hell."

He got so angry at me that he reached across the table and slapped me so hard that it knocked my chair backward, and I fell to the floor. He shouted at me, "Get up, you, stupid idiot! *Get up!*" I got up from the floor, stood my chair back up, and sat back down with strength to endure whatever he was going to do to me. He slapped me again until my face was burning, and I felt a little dizzy. I could feel my eye swelling up as I tried to peruse the room to see if I saw my dad. The man began to yell at me again and said, "You look at me when I am talking to you, young lady! Now, will you denounce this stupid religion and this man you call Jesus and give your allegiance to your real leader?"

I answered yelling back at him, "I refuse to give my allegiance to anybody but my Lord!"

I could hear guards and those in all black all over the room yelling and screaming at my fellow Christians who were being grilled and questioned about their faith as well. The guard began to yell at me again, "Okay, I am going to ask you one more time, will you denounce this man you call Jesus and give your allegiance to the real savior?"

I vehemently yelled back at him, "I will not! I will not! I believe in Jesus Christ as my Savior who died for the sins of the whole world."

He reached across the table and slapped me again even harder. This time, he busted my bottom lip and said he was going to wear me down. I told him, "I don't care how much you yell at me and hit me. I will not bow down to the Antichrist, and I refuse to take the *mark*."

As I glanced around the room I was disturbed because I saw some of the people being slapped and tortured. Some of the men in black had some type of torch or lighters in their hands and was burning the fingertips of some of the people they were questioning. The other guards looked on with sinister smiles on their faces.

The Christians who were being tortured were screaming in pain, and to my horror, a small amount of them began to cave in and took the *mark*. I could hear the machines on the tables revving up to give them the *mark*, which sealed their fate.

I began to remember all of the things my mom had warned me about, all of the Bible studies that I had with my dad, and the preached word from Pastor Goodman, so I was not afraid to die.

Timothy walked back to the microphone to give instructions to the men and women in black and began to speak, "All right, everyone, settle down! My dear faithful men of valor, you have done your job tonight, and I commend you for a job well done. Some of these poor misguided people came to their senses and denounced this foolish religion. Trust me, they will be rewarded. Let's get them lined up so we can put them on the buses that we have parked out front. We are going to take them where they will be assigned their new jobs working for our leader."

I felt so sorry for them as they were led out of the room with shame written on their faces. Some of them were crying and would not even look at those of us who stood firm in our faith; they just kept their heads down as they walked behind the guards. The good news was that the majority of us did not cave under the pressure. I didn't see my dad, Pastor Goodman, Brother Willie, Sister Betty, my cellmates, nor any of our campers walking in that line of shame.

Timothy then gave orders for the rest of us to be taken back to our cells, "I assure all of you that we are going to break you down one way or another." I was glad that they were finished with us for the night. I was so tired and hungry. Plus, the left side of my face, my eye, and my bottom lip had swollen up.

They walked all of us back to our cells, pushing some of us in anger. A couple of times, I was pushed down to the floor and was kicked because I was accused of walking too slow.

When I finally got back to my cell, Sister Betty and Pebbles were already in there, but I didn't see Sister Margaret. When the guard closed and locked the bars, I made sure that he was far down the hall, and the three of us hugged and cried in each other's arms. I asked them where Sister Margaret was. They both looked at each other with sad looks on their faces. Sister Betty told me that she couldn't take the pressure and the torture, and she caved in. A flood of tears welled up in my eyes because I knew what was going to be her fate.

Sister Betty was holding her hand as if she were in pain. I asked her if she was all right and to let me see her hand. She showed me her fingertips, and they were burned at the tips, and some of her fingers were bleeding. She had a big knot on the side of her head where she had been beaten with the baton. Pebbles had been punched in the nose, and she had dried-up blood on it. We all grabbed each other, and Sister Betty began to pray, "Dear Lord Jesus, we thank you for sending your Holy Spirit to give us strength today in our hour of trial and uncertainty. We thank you for sparing our lives. We pray that whatever we have to face tomorrow, we will be strong and stand up for our faith, in Jesus's name. Amen."

After we prayed, I went over to the sink and got one of the towels hanging on the rack and ran it under the faucet until warm water came out. I squeezed out the water and walked over to Sister

Betty and began to tend to her burned fingers. Pebbles leaned over the sink and scooped up some water in her hands and began to wash the blood from her nose. After I tended to Sister Betty's wounds, I placed the towel back under the warm water, rung it out, and held the towel on the side of my face and eye.

After we all tended to our wounds, Sister Betty and Pebbles told me that we all needed to go to bed early and get some rest because we were going to need our strength for whatever we had to face the next day. I climbed in the top bunk hungry and exhausted as I laid my head on my pillow. I stared up at the ceiling almost numb from the ordeal we had gone through.

After I lay in my bed for what seemed to be a couple of hours, I reached inside of my pillowcase, took out my journal, and wrote about everything that we had gone through today. I began thanking God for giving me "holy boldness," and I shed a few tears for Sister Margaret as I wrote.

CHAPTER 15

THE DREADED ANNOUNCEMENT

This morning, when I woke up, I felt an urgency to take my journal with us wherever we were going; so once again, I hid it in my underpants. As we were being led to the lunchroom by our guard, Debbie, for breakfast, I noticed that she was unusually quiet. She had a sad look on her face. I asked her if she was all right, and she started looking around as if she was afraid someone was watching or listening. As we were being led down the hallway, we approached an opening of a door. When we got close to it, I noticed that it was the laundry room. Debbie looked around again and then whispered, "Quick, hurry up and duck in this room. I need to talk to you, and we don't have much time." We followed her directions and ducked into the room. It had huge industrial-sized washing machines, and I could see clothes and suds swirling around in four of them. There were also industrial-sized dryers that were drying clothes. The sounds were so loud that we could barely hear anyone talking.

Debbie pulled us into a circle and closed the door behind us. She began to talk to us, "I don't have much time, so listen, I need to say this quick. This room is the only room in this camp where it is not bugged because of the noise of these machines.

"I am a Christian just like you all. I was the one who placed that Bible tract under your table so that you would be strengthened in your faith. Timothy and the rest of the crew think that I am one of them. I faked getting the *mark*. There are a few of us here in hiding to help our fellow Christians to survive.

"I want to warn you that, today, they are going to give each of you one more chance to deny your faith. You are going to be forced to watch another message from Benetue Commeme. His message is that he is ordering all Christians to be killed today if they do not take the *mark*. They are going to start with the men, then the women, and the young people last. I heard this information last night.

"Several of us Christian guards have vowed to warn you and to encourage you to take a stand for Christ. Please don't cave in, even if it means death. We all know that the Bible says, 'To be absent from the body is to be present with the Lord.' This is our assignment from God to encourage you as you make that final journey. As for me, if I get caught, I am ready to die as well."

She motioned for us to hold hands, and we all prayed for each other. She then walked over to the door and opened it slowly. She peered out of it to see if the coast was clear and motioned for us to hurry up and go out.

Debbie led us down the hallway back to the cafeteria, and we did our usual routine of getting our trays and moving up in the line to be served; however, this time, they only put two slices of bread and a cup of water on our tray. I realized they were trying to starve us because of our refusal to denounce Jesus Christ.

As we walked toward our assigned table, I glanced over to where my dad and Pastor Goodman were sitting. My dad gave me a heart sign with both of his hands, and Pastor Goodman smiled at me. I glanced over at the other table and spotted Brother Willie; he smiled at me and at Sister Betty. I knew that they longed to be with each other during this ordeal. Sister Betty threw him a kiss and pointed her finger up toward heaven as if to tell him to be strong.

We sat down at our assigned tables following their directions to not talk to each other and to keep our heads down as we ate. I was so hungry that I gulped that bread down quickly. The water was at room temperature, but I didn't even care. It was still refreshing just the same.

After we finished eating, we kept our heads down until they ordered us to get up and to form a line against the wall. As we stood in line, they yelled at us to look straight ahead and not to talk and led us out of the cafeteria to the deprogramming room. My heart was racing, and my head was hurting. I began to think, *What are they getting ready to do to us today? Will they kill us?* I prayed, *Oh, Lord, I am in your care. Please give me the strength and the courage to face whatever is getting ready to happen.*

As we were led into the deprogramming room, I noticed that the large screen had been set up. Debbie was right; we were getting ready to hear words from Commeme this morning. Timothy was standing up front with the control to the projector in his hand. When we were all seated, Timothy began to speak, "I know that some of you are tired, hungry, and ready to change your mind about your nonsense. We brought you here today so that you can hear from our leader as he encourages you to do the right thing and surrender." He pushed the button of the remote control, and it projected a live message from Dr. Benetue Commeme on the screen and began to speak:

"Ladies and gentlemen, it is with sincere pleasure and joy that I am able to speak to you all over the world today. The majority of leaders all over the world have surrendered their allegiance and power to me. They have recognized that I am the chosen one. I am the redeemer of mankind, and all must surrender to me.

"However, there is a small fraction of foolish people who has been resistant to the new world order and refuse to renounce their Christian beliefs. They are still trying to spread their hate and their misinformation to you. Please, don't believe them because it is a lie. It is with deep sadness and regret that I must order that these poor misguided people be put to death. The universal higher power has directed me to do so.

"So today, we are giving you one more chance to surrender and join us by taking my *mark*, which will show your allegiance to me. It is a very painless procedure, and it will be done quickly. Then, we will assign you to one of our workstations for your new job.

"I trust that you will make this decision and join us!"

Timothy walked back over to the front of the room and picked up the remote from the table in front and turned off the projector. He then just stood there for a while, scanning the room with a mean and demonic look on his face. He ordered the men in black to gather each one of us and line us up against the wall. So the men in black began dragging us to those tables again with the machines that gave the *mark of the beast.*

I had a nervous stomach. It felt like I was about to throw up; however, I kept encouraging myself in the Lord. As I was led to one of the tables, I glanced and saw our guard, Debbie, looking at me. She took her finger and put it on her chin and lifted it up as if to tell me to keep my chin up and be brave. I nodded back at her and looked around the room to see if I saw Sister Betty, Pebbles, Dad, Brother Willie, and Pastor Goodman, but the man in black in front of me began the usual drill. "What is your name, and what is your decision? Will you denounce Jesus Christ and give your allegiance to the true leader, Benetue Commeme?" I answered him, "My name is Stacie Wilson, and I am a Christian. I refuse to give my allegiance to the Antichrist."

The guard began to stare at me with pure hatred. He took his fist and punched me right in my nose. It began to bleed, and he grabbed my arm and tried to put it in that machine. I snatched my arm back out and wiped the blood from my nose and repeatedly said, "I refuse to surrender! I refuse to surrender! I don't care what you do to me. My God is waiting for me on the other side of death." Then I began to recite Psalm 23 with strength and holy boldness:

The LORD is my shepherd; I shall not want. He maketh me to lie down in green pastures: he leadeth me beside the still waters. He restoreth my soul: he leadeth me in the paths of righteousness for his name's sake. Yea, though I walk through the valley of the shadow of death, I will fear no evil: for thou art with me; thy rod and thy staff they comfort me. Thou preparest a table before me in the

presence of mine enemies: thou anointest my head
with oil; my cup runneth over. Surely goodness
and mercy shall follow me all the days of my life:
and I will dwell in the house of the LORD forever.[17]

The guard slapped me again and then stood up and paced back
and forth in front of the table in total anger and disbelief that he
could not get me to surrender. He motioned for one of the other
guards to come and assist him. When the guard came over to the
table, they talked with each other, and the man walked over to tell
Timothy to come over to our table.

Timothy was going from table to table getting right in the faces
of the people who were being persuaded to denounce their faith.
When the guard walked over to him and whispered in his ear, he
pointed toward our table, and Timothy walked over to us and began
to stare at me.

The guard who was interrogating me told him that I refused to
surrender. Timothy said, "I know this girl, she was one of the ones at
the camp I was assigned to. I know how to persuade her to surrender.
I will round up her family, her pastor, and all of those people from
her camp. We are going to lead them up the hill and give them one
last chance to stop this foolishness once and for all."

He ordered the guard to get me up from the chair, and he walked
over to the microphone and made an announcement. "Attention,
guards! I want you to round up everybody from the Goodman Camp.
You will know who they are by their numbers on their uniform. It
should begin with the letter G, which stands for Goodman, and then
a number."

The next thing I knew, the guards started running up and down
the room checking everyone's numbers on their uniforms. Then one by
one, they rounded all of my family and church members up. I screamed
as I called out for my dad, "Daddy! Daddy!" He was in line in front of
me, and I ran and grabbed him by the waist as we both cried. He held
me tight and wouldn't let go as we were led out of the building.

---

[17] Psalm 23: 1–13 (KJV)

They led us around the back of the barracks to one of the buses that were parked. It was pitch-dark and cold, and I could hardly see where we were going; however, I did notice that our guard, Debbie, was following close behind us and boarded the bus with us. I looked at her, and she nodded and smiled as if to encourage me once again to be strong. I pulled out my journal that I had tucked away in my underpants. I was glad God gave me the unction to bring it with me today. Now I know why. So while we were on the bus, I was writing my final chapter.

The guard cranked up the bus and started driving up a steep hill. Dad reached over and grabbed my face and said, "Honey, I just want you to know that I love you so much. It has been a pleasure having you in my life. God put us together, and I am so glad that you led me to the Lord. I want you to be brave and to know that God is with us." We hugged each other and cried together, not in fear but with a joy that I had never experienced before. We were getting ready to be with our Lord and with our loved ones who had been raptured. I would see my mom and my grandparents very soon.

As the bus climbed up the steep hill, I noticed that there was a platform with several ropes hanging on it. I thought to myself, *They are actually going to hang us on gallows;* however, I wasn't afraid. God had given each one of us the strength to endure this last trial.

Dad was holding my hand, and I looked behind me on the bus and saw Brother Willie and Sister Betty sitting together; they had their heads on each other's shoulder and holding hands as well. I noticed that Pebbles was sitting next to one of the other ladies from our camp, and I could see her lips moving as if she were praying.

Pastor Goodman began to sing, and we all joined in with him singing; and once again, it sounded like the angels joined in with us.

> When peace like a river, attendeth my way,
> When sorrows like sea billows roll;
> Whatever my lot, thou hast taught me to say
> It is well, it is well, with my soul, with my soul
> It is well, (it is well), with my soul!

Then the guard stopped the bus and ordered all of us to get off. As I was finishing my last entry in my journal, Debbie walked up behind me and whispered to me, "Give me your journal, I will finish it for you!" I handed her the journal and began to walk with a smile of victory on my face.

CHAPTER 16

VICTORY

Hello, my name is Debbie Wiley. I am the guard who was assigned to Stacie and the women from her camp. I have been given the awesome privilege of writing the last entry in her journal.

I witnessed a miracle tonight as Stacie; her dad; Brother Willie and his wife, Sister Betty; Pastor Goodman; Stacie's friend Pebbles; and all of the people from their camp were led to gallows to be hanged. I watched prayerfully from a distance as they were being led to the gallows; every one of them had a glow on their faces and were smiling as if the presence of the Holy Spirit was walking right beside them.

Every one of them was (strangely) gazing straight up toward the sky as the guards positioned them into a single row across this huge platform and had them step up on wooden stools that were underneath each noose. They began to place the ropes around their necks, and one of the guards said, "We are giving you one last chance to stop this foolishness and give your allegiance to our leader, Benetue Commeme! Will you denounce your faith and surrender?"

None of them spoke a word but kept their eyes looking upward in the sky. The guard (then) pulled a lever on the platform floor, which made it shift, and all of the wooden stools moved from underneath them. One by one, they began to dangle in the air being held up only by the ropes around their necks. Their feet began to kick violently, and then they stopped. Their bodies became limp as they hung there for a while, and finally, their heads dropped down to their chest.

The guards began to examine each one of them to make sure they were dead. They began cutting the nooses from around their necks and just let their bodies drop down into a dark hole directly underneath them on the platform. At that very moment, God revealed to me that every one of them had actually gotten a glimpse of heaven before they died; that is why they kept gazing up into the sky. *What a beautiful sight that must have been!* I was especially blessed by "Stacie" (the writer of this journal) who was just a teenage girl, and yet she was willing to die for her faith.

To actually witness the martyrdom of these Christians really encouraged me. I was saddened because of this tragedy, but at the same time, I felt blessed to witness the courage of these brave men and women. It gave me a renewed faith to carry out my mission for the Lord of helping and encouraging other Christians brought to this deprogramming camp to keep the faith and to stand strong.

I have had many close calls of being discovered, but so far, God has protected me and the other guards who are believers.

I don't know how long I have before I am discovered as a Christian and be put to death as well. I am going to take this journal back to the barracks and leave it under the table in the cafeteria to be a source of strength and encouragement to the next person.

We all got back on the buses and made the trip back down the hill to the barracks. Some of the guards were having conversations, laughing, and high-fiving each other because they thought they were being loyal to Commeme's orders. Some of us were quiet and reflective of what we had just witnessed.

When we got to the bottom of the hill, the driver parked the bus. I stood up from my seat and began walking behind the guards who were in front of me. I put the journal in my pants pocket so that it wouldn't be noticed.

When we got back inside the building, it was time for us to be debriefed, so we were ordered to meet in the large meeting room where we deprogrammed people. As we all filed in and took our seats. I had a feeling something was about happen. I am sitting here (secretly) documenting in this journal the things that are taking place.

Timothy walked up to the microphone and began speaking to all of us:

"I know it is late in the evening, and many of you are tired from witnessing the deaths of these poor unfortunate people who wouldn't yield to the teachings and beliefs our commander and leader has mandated throughout the world. I want to commend each of you for a job well done. I know it wasn't easy, but you all are some of the best of the best.

"Now, I want to let you know that it has been brought to my attention that there are traitors among us who have been disguising themselves as one of the One Way United force. I was informed that they have counterfeit images of the *mark* on their hands. We are going to examine every guard, kitchen worker, housekeeping staff, and even them on special forces teams. I assure you that we will find you, and you will be put to death as well."

Right now, they are ordering all of us to stand and line up against the wall. I am trying to continue documenting in this journal what is occurring, so I keep it tucked under my left armpit until I can find chances to write.

There are three people ahead of me. My heart is racing, and I am praying, "Holy Spirit, please give me guidance as to where to leave this journal." I am glancing around the room trying to figure out where to leave it. I notice that there are some little shelves underneath the chairs on the left side of me.

I am going to slip out of the line while nobody is paying attention and place the journal underneath the chair on the shelf. So if you happen to find this journal and you are reading it, know that I have been discovered and have met the same fate as Stacie and her family. Don't worry because I am going to be with the Lord. *Remember to be faithful, and may God be*—TO BE CONTINUED…

ABOUT THE AUTHOR

Jynean Elyse Chandler,
BA, DMin, ThD

Dr. Jynean E. Chandler has been a licensed Evangelist Missionary through the Church of God in Christ for over forty-five years. She served as district missionary for the Inspirational District of the Agape Ecclesiastical Jurisdiction (Detroit, Michigan) Church of God in Christ from 2012 to 2015.

She graduated from Mumford High School (Detroit, Michigan) in 1969 and later from Sawyer School of Business (Centerline, Michigan) in 1974, earning a degree in steno-prep. In 2000, she graduated from Logo's Christian College and Graduate Schools (Detroit, Michigan), earning a double major, obtaining her associate's and bachelor's degree in Christian counseling and Christian education.

In 2010, she graduated from Liberty University (Lynchburg, Virginia), earning a master's degree in theological studies. In 2012, she attended Next Dimension University (Rancho Cucamonga, California) where she earned a doctorate of ministry (DMin) degree and later her doctorate of theology (ThD) in 2013.

Dr. Jynean E. Chandler has served as the chancellor of the Bible and Training Institute of Michigan for over eighteen years. The Bible and Training Institute not only offers courses to laymen who wish to further their Christian education by obtaining certificates and diplomas in religious studies. The institute also offers a course of study called the "Ministers and Missionaries Auxiliary Awareness Institute

(MMAAI)" where men and women are trained and prepared to obtain their ministerial licensing within the Church of God in Christ through the Agape Ecclesiastical Jurisdiction as well as working with other aggregations for ministerial training and credentialing.

She is also the dean of the Agape Ecclesiastical Jurisdictional workshops where God has given her the privilege to write all of the lessons as well as organize the workshops for the men and women's classes during the holy convocation, worker's meetings, and the women's conventions.

She is a gospel playwright and has written several musical dramas. She is a puppeteer and created a puppet production company called "The POPs (Puppets of Praise)." She is a Christian writer and author, publishing the following books: *Daily Devotionals for Everyday Christian Living Workbook* and children's book titled *The Handiwork of God*. She also published her first novel titled *Too Late*.

In February 2015, she became the First Lady, assisting her husband in their new ministry at Fellowship Chapel Ministries Church of God in Christ, Detroit, Michigan. *To God be the glory!*